EXTREME RAPID WEIGHT LOSS HYPNOSIS

How to lose weight permanently and without effort. Develop mini habits and increase your motivation to become the best version of yourself

Table of contents

Introduction

Hypnosis is rewiring your brain to add or change your daily routine, starting from your basic instincts. This happens due to the fact that while you are in a hypnotic state, you are more susceptible to suggestions by the person who put you in this state. In the case of self-hypnosis, the person who made you enter the trance of hypnotism is yourself. Thus, the only person who can give you suggestions that can change your attitude in this method is you and you alone.

Again, you must forget the misconception that hypnosis is like sleeping because if it is, then it would be impossible to give autosuggestions to yourself. Try to think about it, like being in a very vivid daydream where you can control every aspect of your situation. This gives you the ability to change anything that may bother and hinder you from achieving the best possible result. If you are able to pull it off properly, then the possibility of improving yourself after the constant practice of the method will just be a few steps away.

Career

People say that motivation is the key to improve in your career. But no matter how you love your career, you must admit that there are aspects of your work that you really do not like doing. Even if it is a fact that you are good at the other tasks, there is that one duty that you dread. And every time you encounter this specific chore, you seem to be slowed down, thus lessening your productivity at work. This is where self-hypnosis comes into play.

The first thing you need to do is find that task you do not like. In some case, there might be multiple of them depending on your personality and how you feel about your job. Now, try to look at why you do not like that task and do simple research on how to make the job a lot simpler. You can then start conditioning yourself to use the simple method every time you do the job.

After you are able to condition your state of mind to do the task, each time you encounter it, it will become the trigger for your trance and thus giving you the ability to perform it better. You will not be able to tell the difference since you will not mind it at all. Your coworkers and superiors will definitely notice the change in your work style and productivity.

Family

It is easy to improve in a career. But to improve your relationship with your family can be a little trickier. Yet, self-hypnosis can still reprogram you to better interact with your family members by modifying how you react to the way they act. You will have the ability to adjust your way of thinking, depending on the situation. This allows you to respond in the most positive way possible, no matter how dreadful the scenario may be.

For example, if you are in a fight with your husband/wife, the normal reaction is to flare up and face fire with fire. This approach usually engulfs the entire relationship, which might eventually lead up to separation. In this instance, being in a hypnotic state can help you think clearly and change the impulse of saying words without thinking through. Anger will still be there, of course; it is a healthy way. But anger now under self-hypnosis can be channeled and stop being a raging inferno;

you can turn it into a steady bonfire that can help you and your partner find common ground for whatever issue you are facing. The same applies to dealing with siblings or children. If you are able to condition your mind to think more rationally or to get into the perspective of others, then you can have better family/friends' relationships.

Health and Physical Activities

Losing weight can be the most common reason why people will use self-hypnosis in terms of health and physical activities. But this is just one part of it. Self-hypnosis can give you a lot more to improve this aspect of your life. It works the same way while working out.

Most people tend to give up their exercise program due to the exhaustion they think they can no longer take. But through self-hypnosis, you will be able to tell yourself that the exhaustion is lessened and allows you to finish the entire routine. Keep in mind that your mind must never be conditioned to forget exhaustion; it must only not mind it until the exercise ends. Forgetting it completely might lead you to not stopping to work out until your energy is depleted. It becomes counterproductive in this case.

Having a healthy diet can also be influenced by self-hypnosis. Conditioning your mind to avoid unhealthy food can be done. Thus, hypnosis will be triggered when you are tempted to eat a meal you are conditioned to consider unhealthy. Your eating habit can then change to benefit you to improve your overall health.

Mental, Emotional, and Spiritual Needs

Since self-hypnosis deals directly with how you think, it is then no secret that it can greatly improve your mental, emotional and spiritual needs. A clear mind can give your brain the ability to have more rational thoughts. Rationality then leads to better decision-making and easy absorption and retention of the information you might need to improve your mental capacity. You must set your expectations, though; this does not work like magic that can turn you into a genius. The process takes time depending on how far you want to go, how much you want to achieve. Thus, the effects will only be limited by how much you are able to condition your mind.

In terms of emotional needs, self-hypnosis cannot make you feel differently in certain situations. But it can condition you to take in each scenario a little lighter and make you deal with them better. Others think that getting rid of emotion can be the best course of action if you are truly able to rewire your brain. But they seem to forget that even though rational thinking is often influenced negatively by emotion, it is still necessary for you to decide on things basing on the common ethics and aesthetics of the real world. Self-hypnosis then can channel your emotion to work in a more positive way in terms of decision making and dealing with emotional hurdles and problems.

Spiritual need, on the other hand, is far easier to influence when it comes to doing self-hypnosis. As a matter of fact, most people with spiritual beliefs are able to do self-hypnosis each time they practice what they believe in. A deep prayer, for instance, is a way to self-hypnotize yourself to enter the trance to feel closer to a Divine existence. Chanting and meditation done by other religions also lead and have the same goal.

Even the songs during a mass or praise and worship trigger self-hypnosis depending if the person allows them to do so.

Still, the improvements can only be achieved if you condition yourself that you are ready to accept them. The willingness to put in an effort must also be there. Effortless hypnosis will only create the illusion that you are improving and thus will not give you the satisfaction of achieving your goal in reality.

How Hypnosis Can Help Resolve Childhood Issues

Another issue that hypnosis can help with is problems from our past. If you have had traumatic situations from your childhood days, then you may have issues in all areas of your adult life. Unresolved issues from your past can lead to anxiety and depression in your later years. Childhood trauma is dangerous because it can alter many things in the brain, both psychologically and chemically.

The most vital thing to remember about trauma from your childhood is that given a harmless and caring environment in which the child's vital needs for physical safety, importance, emotional security, and attention are met, the damage that trauma and abuse cause can be eased and relieved. Safe and dependable relationships are also a dynamic component in healing the effects of childhood trauma in adulthood and make an atmosphere in which the brain can safely start the process of recovery.

Pure hypnoanalysis is the only most effective method of treatment available in the world today for the resolution of phobias, anxiety, depression, fears, psychological and emotional problems/symptoms, and eating disorders. It is a highly advanced form of hypnoanalysis (referred to as analytical hypnotherapy or hypnoanalysis). Hypnoanalysis, in its numerous forms, is practiced all over the world; this method of hypnotherapy can completely resolve the foundation of anxieties in the unconscious mind, leaving the individual free of their symptoms for life.

There is a deeper realism active at all times around us and inside us. This reality commands that we must come to this world to find happiness, and every so often that our inner child stands in our way. This is by no means intentional; however, it desires to reconcile wounds from the past or address damaging philosophies which were troubling to us as children.

Therefore, to disengage the issues that upset us from earlier in our lives, we have to find a way to bond with our internal child; we then need to assist in rebuilding this part of us which will, in turn, help us to be rid of all that has been hindering us from moving on.

Connecting with your inner child may seem like something that may be hard or impossible to do, especially since they may be a part that has long been buried. It is a fairly easy exercise to do and can even be done right now. You will need about 20 minutes to complete this exercise. Here's what you do: find a quiet spot where you won't be disturbed and find a picture of you as a child if you think it may help.

Breathe in and loosen your clothing if you have to. Inhale deeply into your abdomen and exhale, repeat until you feel yourself getting relaxed; you may close your eyes and focus on getting less tense. Feel your forehead and head relax, let your face become relaxed, and relax your shoulders. Allow your body to be limp and loose while you breathe slowly. Keep breathing slowly as you let all of your tension float away.

Now slowly count from 10-0 in your mind and try to think of a place from your childhood. The image doesn't have to be crystal clear right now but try to focus on exactly how you remember it and keep that image in mind. Imagine yourself as a child and imagine observing younger you; think about your clothes, expression, hair etc. In your mind go and meet yourself, introduce yourself to you.

Chapter 1.   What Is Hypnosis?

Hypnosis is a great way to help those in need of weight loss. There are various reasons a person may be overweight. Some may range from behavioral issues or underlying conditions that will require to be addressed to lose weight successfully. After losing weight, a person needs to maintain it.

Does Hypnosis Accelerate Your Weight Loss?

Those that have utilized entrancing to help in weight reduction have revealed incredible enhancements at the speed at which they had the option to shed the pounds. Here, we will talk about how this happens, utilizing suggestions from those that have attempted and succeeded.

Spellbinding is an instrument utilized by certain advisors to help individuals accomplish total unwinding. Specialists believe that the cognizant and oblivious personalities can concentrate on verbal reiteration and mental imaging during a session. As an outcome, the psyche winds up open to recommendations and open to modifying conduct, emotions, and practices.

Since the 1700s, types of this elective treatment have been utilized to help people from bed-wetting to nail-gnawing to smoking with anything. As we will research in this paper, Spellbinding examination has likewise demonstrated some guarantees to treat corpulence.

Mesmerizing might be progressively productive for people who need to get in shape than an eating regimen and exercise alone. The idea is that to change practices like gorging, the psyche can be influenced. Be that as it may, it is as yet being tackled decisively how effective it tends to be.

What's In Store from Hypnotherapy

Clarifying how fascinatingly it works, your specialist will most likely begin your session during the hypnotherapy. At that point, they will go past your private goals. Your specialist can begin talking in an unwinding, delicate tone from that point to help you unwind and make a suspicion that all is well and good.

When you have arrived at an increasingly open perspective, your advisor may propose techniques to help adjust eating or practicing rehearses or different strategies to accomplish your destinations of weight reduction.

With this point, certain words or redundancy of specific sentences can help. Your specialist may likewise help you to envision yourself by trading striking mental symbolism to accomplish targets.

Your advisor will help you escape trance and back to your beginning state to close the session. The term of the mesmerizing session and the total measure of sessions you may need will depend on your targets. In as few as one to three gatherings, a few people may see results.

Types of Hypnotherapy

Different sorts of hypnotherapy exist. For example, for propensities, smoking, nail-gnawing, and dietary issues, recommendation treatment is all the more as often as possible utilized.

With different meds, such as healthful guidance or CBT, your specialist may likewise utilize hypnotherapy.

Hypnotherapy expenses change depending on where you live and the specialist you pick. Think about calling forward to talk about choices for estimating or sliding scale.

Your protection business can cover somewhere in the range of 50 and 80% of affirmed experts' treatment. Call for more data about your inclusion once more.

You can find authorized specialists by mentioning a referral from your essential doctor or via looking through the suppliers ' database of the American Society for Clinical Hypnosis.

Points of interest for Hypnotherapy

Studies demonstrate that a few people might be increasingly responsive and, in this way, bound to profit by the effects of entrancing. For example, an individual might be progressively inclined to mesmerizing by certain character qualities, benevolence, and transparency.

Research has likewise found that mesmerizing helplessness ascends after age 40, and females are progressively plausible to be open, paying little mind to age. Under the direction of an affirmed trance specialist, spellbinding is viewed as a protected practice with not many reactions, for example:

- Headache

- Dizziness

- Drowsiness

- Anxiety trouble

- Fake memory creation

Individuals who are masters in visualizations or daydreams should converse with their primary care physician before psychotherapy is explored. Likewise, affected by drugs or liquor, the mental state ought not to be performed on a private person.

Here are a few things you can do at home to enable you to get more fit:

- Move your body on most days of the week. Attempt to get either 150 minutes of moderate action (for example, strolling, water heart stimulating exercise, cultivating) or 75 minutes of progressively lively workout (for example, running, swimming, climbing) each week.

- Keep a day-by-day dinner. Track the amount you eat, when you eat, and if you eat from yearning or not. Doing so can enable you to recognize evolving propensities, for example, fatigue eating.

- Eat vegetables and natural products. Go for five foods grown from the ground servings consistently. To check your craving, you ought to likewise add more fiber to your eating routine— between 25 to 30 grams every day.

- Drink water each day from six to eight glasses. Being hydrated abstains from eating excessively.

- The inclination to skip suppers is safe. Eating throughout the day keeps up your digestion going incredible.

Chapter 2. Hypnosis and Weight Loss

Hypnosis plays a vital role in medicinal solutions. In modern-day society, it is recommended to treat many different conditions, including obesity or weight loss in overweight individuals.

Once you understand the practice and how it is conducted, you will find that everything makes sense. Hypnosis works for weight loss because of the relationship between our minds and bodies.

Since two of the most significant issues society faces today are media-based influences and a lack of motivation, you can quickly solve any problems related by merely correcting your mind.

Correcting your mind is an entirely different mission on its own, or without hypnosis, that is. It is a challenge that most will get frustrated. Nobody wants to deal with themselves. Although that may be true, perhaps one of the best lessons hypnosis teaches you is the significance of spending time focusing on your intentions. Daily practicing of hypnosis includes focusing on specific ideas. Once these ideas are normalized in your daily routine and life, you will find it easier to cope with struggles and ultimately break bad habits, which is the ultimate goal.

In reality, it takes 21 consecutive days to break a bad habit, but only if a person remains persistent, integrating both a conscious and consistent effort to quit or rectify a practice. It takes the same amount of time to adopt a new healthy habit. With hypnosis, it can take up to three months to either break a bad habit or form a new one. However, even though hypnosis takes longer, it tends to work far more effectively than just forcing yourself to do something you don't want to do.

Our brains are robust operating systems that can be fooled under the right circumstances. Hypnosis has been proven to be useful for breaking habits and adopting new ones due to its powerful effect on the mind. It can be measured in the same line of consistency and power as affirmations. Now, many would argue that hypnosis is unnecessary and that completing a 90-day practice of hypnotherapy to change habits for weight loss is a complete waste of time. However, when you think about someone who needs to lose weight but can't seem to do it, then you might start reconsidering it as a helpful solution to the problem. It's no secret that the human brain requires far more than a little push or single affirmation to thrive. Looking at motivational video clips and reading quotes every day is great, but it helps you move further from A to B?

It's true that today, we are faced with a sense of rushing through life. Asking an obese or unhealthy individual why they gained weight, there's a certainty that you'll receive similar answers.

Could it be that no one has time to, for instance, cook or prep healthy meals, visit the gym or move their bodies? Apart from making up excuses as to why you can't do something, there's actual evidence hidden in the reasons why we sell ourselves short and opt for the easy way out.

Could it be that the majority of individuals have just become lazy?

Regardless of your excuses, reasons, or inabilities, hypnosis debunks the idea that you have to go all out to get healthier. Losing weight to improve your physical appearance has always been a challenge, and although there is no easy way out, daily persistence and 10 to 60 minutes a day of practice could help you lose weight. Not just that, but it can also restructure your brain and help you to develop better habits, which will guide you in experiencing a much more positive and sustainable means of living.

Regardless of the practice or routine you follow at the end of the day, the principle of losing weight always remains the same. You have to follow a balanced diet in proportion with a sustainable exercise routine.

By not doing so is where most people tend to go wrong with their weight loss journeys. It doesn't matter whether it's a diet supplement, weight loss tea, or even hypnosis. Your diet and exercise routine still play an increasingly important role in losing weight and will be the number one factor that will help you to obtain permanent results. There's a lot of truth in the advice, given that there aren't any quick fixes to help you lose weight faster than what's recommended. Usually, anything that promotes standard weight loss, which is generally about two to five pounds a week, depending on your current Body Mass Index (BMI), works no matter what it is. The trick to losing weight doesn't necessarily lie in what you do but instead in how you do it.

When people start with hypnosis, they may be very likely to quit after a few days or weeks, as it may not seem useful or it isn't leading to any noticeable results.

Nevertheless, if you remain consistent with it, eat a balanced diet instead of crash dieting, and follow a simple exercise routine, then you will find that it has a lot more to offer you than just weight loss. Even though weight loss is the ultimate goal, it's essential to keep in mind that lasting results don't occur overnight. There are no quick fixes, especially with hypnosis.

Adopting the practice, you will discover many benefits, yet two of the most important ones are healing and learning how to activate the fat burning process inside of your body.

Hypnosis is not a diet, nor is it a fast-track method to get you where you want to go. Instead, it is a tool used to help individuals reach their goals by implementing proper habits. These habits can help you achieve results by focusing on appropriate diet and exercise. Since psychological issues influence most weight-related issues, hypnosis acts as the perfect tool, laying a foundation for a healthy mind.

Hypnosis is not a type of mind control, yet it is designed to alter your mind by shifting your feelings toward liking something you might have hated before, such as exercising or eating a balanced diet. The same goes for quitting sugar or binge eating. Hypnosis identifies the root of the issues you may be dealing with and works by rectifying them accordingly. Given that it changes your thought pattern, you may also experience a much calmer and relaxed approach to everything you do.

Hypnosis works by maintaining changes made in mind because of neuroplasticity. Consistent hypnotherapy sessions create new patterns in the brain that result in the creation of new habits. Since consistency is the number one key to losing weight, it acts as a solution to overcome barriers in your mind, which most individuals struggle. Hypnosis can also provide you with many techniques to meet different goals, such as gastric band hypnosis, which works by limiting eating habits, causing you to refrain from overeating.

Chapter 3.   Daily Weight Loss Meditation

Meditation is in fashion. As soon as you tell someone that you have a problem, it is a rare occasion when they do not recommend you practice it. It does not matter if the problem is mental or physical.

Sometimes, people's insistence leads us to reject a plan idea. However, would it not be more interesting to ask why so many people agree to advise you the same thing?

Interest in Eastern cultures brought the influence of ideas to the forefront. And they are our existence's nucleus. Nutrition and physical exercise promote our body's optimal working.

Yet, it is also true that when our emotions aren't controlled, the brain secretes substances that affect our body and mind. Therefore, physical sufferings or thoughts that make life difficult for us can appear. In this way, meditation helps to keep us safe.

Meditation Lowered Inflammation Levels

Beyond what happened in mind, they find an inflammation measure lower than before the investigation. It indicates that perception benefits go beyond what would appear. However, the group manager warns that the exact extent of its benefits cannot yet be defined. Nevertheless, the observation is adequate to multiply scientists' efforts in this regard.

It is no longer about Buddhist experiences or self-help customers who can't control. We have evidence. However, intentional meditation enhances our quality of life. Furthermore, the fact that its effects last four months means that it is a long-term practice that benefits us. Given the number of harmful elements to which we are exposed, it seems reasonable to bet on this option without being able to do anything. All this shows us how the first step to improving our health is to listen to our bodies.

It is very unlikely that the effects you notice when introducing a new habit constitute a mere imagination. Therefore, from here, we want to thank the efforts of many people who have defended an alternative lifestyle—another class of medicine.

Even when they have been treated as "enlightened" and a little sane, their constancy and the defense of their values have been translated into a scientific study that has proved them right and from which we will all benefit.

Practicing Anti-Stress Meditation at Home

We know that sometimes it costs. How to combine our daily obligations with that moment of anti-stress meditation? We get up with things to do and arrive at bed with a mind full of those tasks and commitments that must be fulfilled for the following day.

Be careful if the preceding paragraph is an example of what you always live in your day today. It is essential that you know how to organize times and set limits, control all those pressures that do not allow you to get rest.

Ideally, you learn to balance your life. Where you have always the priority of taking care of your health and your emotions. Stress can hurt you a lot, and you should see it as an enemy to dominate and do small to handle it properly. We explain how to practice anti-stress meditation:

Emotional Agenda

Do you keep an agenda in your day-to-day of the things you should do? Of your obligations, appointments, meetings, appointments with teachers of children, or your visit to the doctor?

Do the same with your emotions, with your personal needs. Spend at least one hour or two hours for yourself each day—to do what you like, to be alone, and to practice anti-stress meditation. Your emotions have priority; make a hole in your day today. You deserve it, and you need it.

A Moment of Tranquility

It doesn't matter where it is— in your room, in the kitchen, or a park. You must be calm and surrounded by an environment that is pleasant, placid, and comforting. If you want, put on the music that you like, but you must be alone.

Regulate Your Breathing

Let's now take care of our breathing. Once you are comfortable, start to take a deep breath through your nose. Allow your chest to swell, then let this air out little by little through your mouth. If you repeat it six or seven times, you will begin to notice a comforting tingling through your body, and you feel better and calmer.

Focus Thoughts

What will we do after? Visualize those pressures that concern you most. Are you pressured at work? Do you have problems with your partner? Visualize those images and keep breathing. The tension should soften, the nerves should lose their intensity, and the fear will soften. You will feel better little by little.

Positive Images

Once you have focused on those images, what more pressure they cause on your being, let's now visualize pleasant things, aspects that you would like to be living, and that would make you happy.

They must be simple things: a walk on the beach, you touching the bark of a tree, you walk through a quiet city where the sun illuminates your face and where the rumor of nearby coffee shops envelops you with a pleasant smell of coffee... Easy things make you happy. Visualize it and keep breathing deeply.

The Silence

Now we close our eyes—At least for two minutes. Try not to think about anything; just let the silence envelop you. You are at peace, and you are well; there is no pressure. There are only you and a quiet world where there are no pressures and threats, and everything is warm and pleasant.

Open Your Eyes in a Renewed Way

It is time to open your eyes and breathe normally again. Look around without moving, without getting up. Don't do it, or you'll run the risk of getting dizzy. Allow about five minutes to pass before you walk again. Surely you feel much better, lighter, and without any pressure on your body.

New Perspectives

Now that you feel more relaxed, try to think about what you can do to find yourself better day-by-day. Being a little happier sometimes requires that we have to make small changes, and the good thing about anti-stress meditation is that it is slowly changing us inside.

It requires us to make small changes to find the balance so that the body and the mind feel in tune again, and the pressures and the anxieties go out of our body like the smoke that escapes through a window.

Simple Meditation Exercises

Stress accumulates like oil. Paradoxically, as one increases, the other declines. Therefore, stress and energy can fuel a wide variety of sources. For example, stress may feed on problems in various places or simply a life pattern marked by a lack of breaks. We will present simple meditation exercises to help relieve this stress.

Indeed, meditation encourages self-awareness. It is an ancient Indian peculiar millennial technique, popular in Buddhist and Hindu beliefs. It's become common in the West in recent years.

Some of the advantages of meditation are an increase in focus, which is the starting point for many other advantages, such as better memory. This also usually enables physical and emotional relaxation. This may also improve our immune system against threats to our safety.

Without further explanation, let's add a set of basic meditation exercises that we can put into action to optimize its benefits.

Focus Your Attention on Breathing

The first of the simple meditation exercises is also one of the easiest to incorporate into our routine. We will do it more easily if we can adopt a relaxed position with semi-open eyes.

It is also good to focus on our breathing without trying to vary the parameters. It's about perceiving the air coming in and going out. At this moment, it is common to be distracted by different thoughts. Our mission will be to ignore them until they lose their strength.

Countdown

This technique is extremely simple and is of great use when it comes to meditating. With your eyes closed, count back from high numbers such as 50 or 100 until you reach zero. The goal of this practice is to focus our attention on a single thought/activity. In this way, we will be able to eliminate the sensations produced by the rest of the stimulations.

Scan Our Own Body

This is the most interesting one of many and simple meditation exercises. We only need to reassess the different parts of our bodies. For this, it is recommended to place ourselves in a place of weak stimulation. Then we will focus our attention on all parts of our body, starting from the head to finish with the feet.

We can contract and release the different muscle groups to become aware of their presence and their movement. It is a rather attractive way to observe ourselves and perceive in detail the sensations of our body.

Observe Dynamically

This exercise is focused on studying our climate. Let's start with a comfortable position; the best is sitting with your eyes closed. We'll then open them to close them for a moment. Before that, we'll have to focus on what's learned.

We'll be able to think about the various sensations that we're generating the stimulations that came to us. We may list them; think of each object's shapes and colors or name. Furthermore, it might be a good way to experience our home differently if we know this at home.

Meditating in Motion

Another basic meditation exercise we can put into action is based on our body's feedback of fun stimuli as it moves. For this, interaction with nature is recommended.

For example, we can take a few steps on the beach or in the woods, enjoy the warmth of the sun on our face, the wind caresses, or the touch of plants and water on our hands. It can also be another way to make a personal observation, thinking about our body's movements as we walk.

Meditate with Fire

Finally, we can use fire as a symbolic purification item to focus our meditation. We may concentrate on a campfire in nature or something simpler: a candle's flame. It will allow us to experience the heat sensations associated with fire and the shadows reflecting on the surrounding objects.

On the other side, we can list and burn negative items in our everyday lives. This positive gesture that can be performed symbolically or factually helps us free ourselves from our worries of something we have no influence over.

Chapter 4.   Actual Self-Hypnotic Suggestions

If you can afford to undergo a series of hypnotherapy sessions with a specialist, you may do so. This is ideal as you will work with a professional who can guide you through the treatment and will also provide you with valuable advice on nutrition and exercises.

Clinical Hypnotherapy

When first meeting with a therapist, they start by explaining the type of hypnotherapy they are using. Then you will discuss your personal goals so the therapist can better understand your motivations.

The formal session will start with your therapist speaking in a gentle and soothing voice. This will help you relax and feel safe during the entire therapy.

Once your mind is more receptive, the therapist will start suggesting ways that can help you modify your exercise or eating habits as well as other ways to help you reach your weight loss goals.

Specific words or repetition of particular phrases can help you at this stage. The therapist may also help you in visualizing the body image you want, which is one effective technique in hypnotherapy.

The therapist will bring you out from the hypnotic stage to end the session, and you will start to be more alert. Your personal goals will influence the duration of the hypnotherapy sessions as well as the number of total sessions that you may need. Most people begin to see results in as few as two to four sessions.

DIY Hypnotherapy

If you are not comfortable working with a professional hypnotherapist or can't afford the sessions, you can choose to perform self-hypnosis. While this is not as effective as the sessions under a professional, you can still try it and see if it can help you with your weight loss goals.

Here are the steps if you wish to practice self-hypnosis:

1. **Believe in the power of hypnotism**. Remember, this alternative treatment requires the person to be open and willing. It will not work for you if your mind is already set against it.
2. **Find a comfortable and quiet room to practice hypnotherapy**. Ideally, you should find a place that is free from noise and where no one can disturb you. Wear loose clothes and set relaxing music to help in setting up the mood.
3. **Find a focal point**. Choose an object in a room that you can focus on. Use your concentration on this object so you can start clearing your mind of all thoughts.
4. **Breathe deeply.** Start with five deep breaths, inhaling through your nose and exhaling through your mouth.
5. **Close your eyes**. Think about your eyelids becoming heavy, and just let them close slowly.
6. **Imagine that all stress and tension are coming out of your body**. Let this feeling move down from your head, to your shoulders, to your chest, to your arms, to your stomach, to your legs, and finally to your feet.
7. **Clear your mind.** When you are relaxed, your account must be clear, and you can initiate the process of self-hypnotism.

8. **Visualize a pendulum**. In your mind, picture a moving swing. The movement of the pendulum is popular imagery used in hypnotism to encourage focus.
9. **Start visualizing your ideal body image and size**. This should help you instill in your subconscious the importance of a healthy diet and exercise.
10. **Suggest to yourself to avoid unhealthy food and start exercising regularly**. You can use a particular mantra such as "I will exercise at least three times a week. Unhealthy food will make me sick."
11. **Wake up**. Once you have achieved what you want during hypnosis, you must wake yourself. Start by counting back from one to 10 and wake up when you reach 10.

Remember, a healthy diet doesn't mean that you have to reduce your food intake significantly. Just cut your consumption of food that is not healthy for you. Never hypnotize yourself out of eating. Only suggest to yourself to eat less of the food that you know is just making you fat.

Chapter 5. Mindful Eating Benefits

There are various scopes of cautious eating techniques, some of them established in Zen and different kinds of Buddhism, others connected to yoga.

My careful eating procedure is figuring out how to be cautious. Rather than eating carelessly, putting nourishment unknowingly in your mouth, not tasting the sustenance you eat, you see your thoughts and feelings.

- Learn to be cautious: why you want to eat and what emotions or requirements can trigger eating?

- What you eat and whether it's reliable.

- Look, smell, taste; feel the nourishment that you eat.

- How do you feel when you taste it, how would you digest it, and go about your day?

- How complete you are previously, during, and in the wake of eating.

- During and in the wake of eating, how are your sentiments?

- Where the nourishment originated from, who could have developed it, the amount it could have suffered before it killed, whether it naturally developed, the amount it was handled, the amount it was broiled or overcooked, and so on.

This is an ability that you don't merely increase medium-term, a type of reflection. It takes practice, and there will be times when you neglect to eat mindfully, begin, and stop. However, you can generally get excellent at this with exercise and consideration.

Mindful Eating Benefits

The upsides of eating are unimaginable, and realizing these points of interest is fundamental as you think about the activity:

- When you're anxious, you figure out how to eat and stop when you're plunking down.

- You figure out how to taste nourishment and acknowledge great sustenance tastes.

- You start to see that unfortunate nourishment isn't as delicious as you accepted, nor does it make you feel extremely pleasant.

- Because of the over three points, if you are overweight, you will regularly get more fit.

- You start arranging your nourishment and eating through the passionate issues you have. It requires somewhat more, yet it's essential.

- Social overeating can turn out to be less of an issue—you can eat while mingling, rehearsing, and not over-alimenting.

- You begin to appreciate the experience of eating more, and as an outcome, you will acknowledge life more when you are progressively present.

- It can transform into a custom of mindfulness that you anticipate.

- You learn for the day how nourishment impacts your disposition and vitality.

- You realize what fuels your training best with nourishment, and you work and play.

A Guide to Mindful Eating

Keeping up a contemporary, quick-paced way of life can leave a brief period to oblige your necessities. You are moving, always starting with one thing then onto the next, not focusing on what your psyche or body truly needs. Rehearsing mindfulness can help you to comprehend those necessities.

When eating mindfulness is connected, it can help you recognize your examples and practices while simultaneously standing out to appetite and completion related to body signs.

You were originating from the act of pressure decrease dependent on mindfulness, rehearsing mindfulness. At the same time, eating can help you focus on the present minute instead of proceeding with ongoing and unacceptable propensities.

Careful eating is an approach to begin an internal looking course to help you become increasingly aware of your nourishment association and utilize that information to eat with joy.

The body conveys a great deal of information and information, so you can start settling on conscious choices instead of falling into programmed—and regularly feeling driven—practices when you apply attention to eating knowledge. You are better prepared to change your conduct once you become aware of these propensities.

Individuals that need to be cautious about sustenance and nourishment are asked to:

- Explore their inward knowledge about food—different preferences.

- Choose sustenance that pleases and supports their bodies.

- Accept explicit sustenance inclinations without judgment or self-analysis.

- Practice familiarity with the indications of their bodies beginning to eat and quit eating.

General Principles of Mindful Eating

One methodology for careful eating depends on the core values given by Rebecca J. Frey, Ph.D., and Laura Jean Cataldo, RN: tune in to the internal craving and satiety signs of your body identifies own triggers for careless eating; for example, social weights, incredible sentiments, and explicit nourishments.

Here are a couple of tips for getting you started:

- **Start with one meal**. It requires some investment to begin with any new propensity. It very well may be challenging to make cautious eating rehearses regularly. However, you can practice with one dinner or even a segment of a supper. Attempt to focus on appetite signs and sustenance choices before you start eating or sinking into the feelings of satiety toward the part of the arrangement—these are unique approaches to begin a routine with regards to consideration.

- **Remove view distractions place or turn off your phone in another space**. Mood killers such as the TV and PC and set away whatever else; for example, books, magazines, and papers—that can divert you from eating. Give the feast before your complete consideration.

- **Tune in your perspective when you start this activity, become aware of your attitude**. Perceive that there is no right or off base method for eating, yet only unmistakable degrees of eating background awareness. Focus your consideration on eating sensations. When you understand that your brain has meandered, take it delicately back to the eating knowledge.

- **Draw in your senses with this activity.** There are numerous approaches to explore. Attempt to investigate one nourishment thing utilizing every one of your faculties. When you put sustenance in your mouth, see the scents, surfaces, hues, and flavors. Attempt to see how the sustenance changes as you cautiously bite each nibble.

- **Take as much time as necessary.** Eating includes backing off, enabling your stomach-related hormones to tell your mind that you are finished before overeating. It's a fabulous method to hinder your fork between chomps. Additionally, you will be better prepared to value your supper experience, especially if you're with friends and family.

Rehearsing mindfulness in a bustling globe can be trying now and again; however, by knowing and applying these essential core values and techniques, you can discover approaches to settle your body all the more promptly. When you figure out how much your association with nourishment can adjust to improve things, you will be charmingly astounded—and this can significantly affect your general prosperity and wellbeing.

Formal dinners, be that as it may, will, in general, assume a lower priority about occupied ways of life for generally people. Instead, supper times are an opportunity to endeavor to do each million stuff in turn. Consider having meals at your work area or accepting your Instagram fix over breakfast to control a task.

The issue with this is you are bound to be genuinely determined in your decisions about healthy eating and overeat on the off chance that you don't focus on the nourishment you devour or the way you eat it.

That is the place mindfulness goes in. You can apply similar plans to a yoga practice straight on your lunch plate. *"Cautious eating can enable you to tune in to the body's information of what, when, why, and the amount to eat,"* says Lynn Rossy, Ph.D., essayist of The Mindfulness-Based Eating Solution and the Center for Mindful Eating director. *"Rather than relying upon another person (or an eating routine) to reveal to you how to eat, developing a minding association with your own body can achieve tremendous learning and change."*

From the ranch to the fork, you can help you conquer enthusiastic eating, make better nourishment choices, and even experience your suppers in a crisp, ideally better way. To make your next dinner mindful, pursue these measures.

Chapter 6.   What Is Emotional Eating?

As even non-professionals eventually come to notice, mental and physical illnesses are categorized by various qualifiers among members of the healthcare professions, such as "disease" (i.e., Lyme disease), "condition" (i.e., psychological condition), and "syndrome" (i.e., toxic-shock syndrome), but few laymen understand the distinctions. Nonetheless, it is quite essential to know how this categorization pertains to this eating "disorder," as it brings clarification to how science views this illness and how the treatment is meant to affect it.

Despite the many physical aspects associated with BED (physical comorbidities), binge-eating disorder is regarded as a psychological rather than physical ailment (an aberrant social behavior), best managed by psychological therapy. That is not to say that medical doctors and other therapeutic practitioners cannot help alleviate many of the symptoms associated with binge-eating disorder, only that such approaches treat the symptoms, not the source(s) of the problem. Thus the first step to understanding binge-eating disorder is to acknowledge that you are dealing with a severe psychological issue—that manifests physically.

Do You Suffer from Emotional Eating?

Obesity levels amongst people are certainly higher than they have ever been in history. This trend has spread throughout the world. People are gaining weight at excessive rates. But the big question is, why? What is it that is causing people to gain weight?

The quick answer is to blame it on junk food, and that would be the logical answer. Many food-manufacturing companies are creating junk foods that are not healthy for people to consume.

Junk foods are processed foods that have been altered from their natural state. Common junk foods contain added pesticides, preservatives, flavorings, sugars, salts, seasonings, and all kinds of things that are bad for our health.

Unnatural foods will cause you to feel strange. In other words, they will cause you to feel symptoms of stress, anxiety, irritation, irregular heartbeat, and more.

Even though these symptoms may be natural in some life circumstances, when they are caused merely by food, then they are unnatural.

The Real Reason

We know junk food is a problem for the majority of health problems in America and other developed countries. Until government agencies ban junk foods from being sold in the supermarkets, they are always going to be there, and people will still buy them.

It is no surprise to ordinary citizens that junk food is bad for them when they see it in the supermarkets. They know cookies, cakes, pizza, and fried foods are just going to make them feel lousy after they eat them. But they continue to eat these foods anyway. So again, why?

The real reason has to do with stress more than anything else. People live such stressful lives in the modern age. They have to worry about making a living, taking care of their kids, and so on. It gets to a point where they have no time to relax and feel comfortable at all.

People in stressful situations tend to form bad habits to relieve their stress. One of the most significant habits people develop is binge eating on junk food.

Once this happens, the unnatural chemicals and additives in those foods will raise their stress levels even higher. So instead of treating the problem, junk food makes it worse.

Control the Eating

You must understand the difference between emotional eating and regular eating. For example, if you are on a strict diet and you can control what you eat, this is proper eating.

When someone eats to relieve their stress and anxiety, this is emotional eating. Even someone who regularly sticks to a healthy diet regime could find themselves eating if they are stressed. This is the inner demon that you have to learn to fight.

So, how does someone gain the discipline to control their eating under stressful situations? The first step is to try and distance yourself from all unhealthy foods.

This means no filling your kitchen cupboards with junk food from the supermarket. Only fill your house with healthy eating. After all, if there are no healthy foods in your home, then you won't be tempted to cheat.

Now, if you are away from your house, like at work, then you might find vending machines nearby that will tempt you into eating poorly. These are always hard to resist someone under distress.

Fortunately, you can eat certain types of foods beforehand that will help limit your cravings to relieve stress pains.

- Avocados — These are fruits that contain folic acid and vitamin B6. These nutrients have been scientifically proven to reduce stress levels by helping the central nervous system function well. It also contains potassium, which regulates blood pressure.

- Salmon — This type of fish is very high in omega-3 fatty acids, which can elevate you into a good mood. These acids also keep your heart healthy, especially if your cortisol levels are high. These stress hormones get released under pressure and cause damage to your heart if they remain elevated. Omega-3s will prevent this.

- Broccoli — This vegetable is a good source of Vitamin C, which is what strengthens the immune system. When you feel stress and anxiety, it can put a burden on your immune system. It will even make you susceptible to colds and flu bugs.

- Almonds — These nuts are loaded with magnesium, which is a mineral that lowers cortisol levels. This will calm down the nervous system when it starts feeling stressed out. You will even sleep better as a result of eating these, which will then help you in other ways as well.

These are the four foods you should have on hand with you at all times, whether you are at work, school, or wherever.

Two of these foods are so simple to carry that you don't even need to cook them.

As for the salmon and broccoli, cook them beforehand and then bring them with you in a Tupperware container.

Now, every time you start feeling stressed out during the day, go ahead and eat a little bit of these foods. You don't necessarily have to eat bites from all of them, although that wouldn't hurt. If you are under time constraints and don't have time to eat, then almonds would be the best food to munch on.

Almonds are hard food and can conveniently be eaten from your desk at work or anywhere. Since they lower cortisol levels, this will ultimately be what you need to keep your stress under control. Then when you have your next lunch break, go ahead and eat the rest of the foods to calm yourself further down.

Now you can still eat other fruits and vegetables if these mood friendly foods don't fill you up. But remember to stay away from all processed foods because they will reverse the positive feelings you have already endured from healthier mood foods.

Eventually, you will start to develop a habit of controlling your mood through healthy eating every time you feel stressed out. Then it will become a routine for you, which means you will have successfully turned a bad habit into a good one.

Chapter 7.   Stopping Emotional Eating

Emotional eating occurs typically when your food becomes a tool that you use in responding to any internal or external emotional cues. It's normal for human beings to react to any stressful situation and the painful feelings they have. Whenever you have stressful emotions, you tend to run after a bag of chips or bars of chocolate, a large pizza, or a jar of ice cream to distract yourself from that emotional pain. The foods that you crave at that moment are referred to as comfort food. Those foods contain a high calorie or high carbohydrate with no nutritional value.

Do you know that your appetite increases whenever you are stressed, and whenever you're stressed, you tend to make poor eating habits? Stress is associated with weight gain and weight loss. You tend to cleave unto food when you are under intense pressure and intense emotions like boredom or sadness. Now that's emotion napping, and it is the way that your body relieves itself from the stress and gets the energy needed to overcome its over-dependence on food. Usually, get you to the point whereby you don't eat healthy anymore.

Emotional eating is a chronic issue that affects every gender, both male and female, but researches have shown that women are more prone to emotional eating than men. Emotional eaters tend to incline towards salty, sweet, fatty, and generally high-calorie foods. Usually, these foods are not healthy for the body, and even if you choose to eat them, you should only consume them with moderation. Emotional eating, especially indulging in unhealthy food, ends up affecting your weight.

Emotional eating was defined as eating in response to intense, passionate emotions. Many studies reveal that having a positive mood can reduce your food intake, so you need to start accepting the fact that positive emotions are now part of emotional eating in the same way that negative emotions are part of emotional eating.

Effects of Emotional Eating

So here are some effects of emotional eating:

Intense Nausea

When you are food binging, the food provides a short-term distraction to the emotions you are facing, and more than often, you will tend to eat very quickly, and as a result, you will overeat. This will then result in stomach pains or nausea, which can last for one or two days. So it is essential to concentrate on the problem that is causing you stress, instead of eating food to solve that problem.

Feeling Guilty

The next one is feeling guilty. Occasionally, you may use food as a reward to celebrate something that is not necessarily bad. It is essential to celebrate the little wings that you have in life, and if food is the way you choose to celebrate it, you should want to eat healthy meals instead of going for unhealthy snacks. However, when food becomes your primary coping mechanism for dealing with emotional stress every time, you feel stressed, upset, lonely, angry, or exhausted. You'll open the refrigerator and find yourself in an unhealthy cycle without even being able to target the root cause of the problem that's stressing you out.

Furthermore, you will be filled with guilt. Even after all the emotional damage has passed away, you will still be filled with remorse for what you have done and the unhealthy lifestyle you choose to make at that moment, which will lower your self-esteem. And then, you will go into another emotional eating outburst.

Weight-Related Health Issues

The next one is weight-related health issues. I'm sure that you are aware of how unhealthy eating affects your weight. Many researchers have discovered that emotional eating affects weight both positively and negatively. Generally, the foods you crave during those emotional moments are high in sugar and high in salt and saturated fats. And in those emotional moments, you tend to eat anything that you can lay your hands on.

Even though some healthy fast foods are available, many are still filled with salt, sugar, and trans-fat content. High carbohydrate food increases the demand for insulin in the body, which then promotes hunger more and more, and therefore you tend to eat more calories than you are supposed to consume. Consuming a high level of fat can have an immediate impact on your blood vessels, and it does that in the short-term. If you drink too much fat, your blood pressure will increase, and you will become hospitable to heart attack, kidney disease, and another cardiovascular disease. Many manufactured fats are created during food processing, and those fat are found in pizza, dough, crackers, fried pies, cookies, and pastries.

Do not be misinformed; no amount of saturated fat is healthy. If you continue to eat this kind of food, you'll be putting yourself at HDL and LDL risks, which are the right kind of cholesterol and the wrong kind of cholesterol. And to be frank, both of them will put your heart at risk of diabetes, high blood pressure, high cholesterol, obesity, and insulin resistance. So these are some of the challenges that you will face when you engage in emotional eating outbursts.

How to Stop Emotional Eating Using Meditation

You already know what to eat, and you already know what is not to eat, and you already know what is right for your body and what is not suitable for your organization. Even if you're not a nutritionist or a health coach, or a fitness activist, you already know these things. But when you are alone, you tend to engage in emotional eating, and you successfully keep it to yourself and make sure that no one knows about it. It is just like you surrender your control for food to a food demon, and when that demon possesses you, you become angry, sad, and stress at once and before you know what is happening, you have gone to your fridge, opened it, and begin to consume whatever is there.

As strong as you, once this food demon has possessed you, it will convince you that food is the only way to get out of that emotional turmoil that you are facing. So before you know what is happening, you are invading your refrigerator and consuming that jar of almond butter that you promised yourself not to drink. And just a few seconds, you open the jar of almond butter, take the bottle, put it in your mouth, and close the door again. And you do it again and again and again, and before you know what is happening, you have leveled the jar up to halfway, and not a dent has been made on the initial in motion that you were eating over.

Now before you know it, if your consciousness catches up with you. You start to feel sad, guilt, and shame. The almond butter that you were eating didn't help you that much, not in the way that you wanted it to help you. So if there is anything you need to realize, you now feel worse than you were one hour ago. And so you make a promise that you won't repeat this again and that this is the last time that this will happen.

You promised yourself never to share an entrance with that almond butter again, but then you realize that this is what you have been doing to the gluten-free cookies, to that ice cream, and hot chocolate before now. If this is your behavior, then you'll be able to relate to this. Emotional eating is a healthy addition that you must stop. It is more of a habit and one not easy to control. So there is hope for you if you are engaging in emotional eating today. You have to be able to have control over yourself and your emotional eating. You can use many strategies to combat emotional eating, and one of them is meditation.

Now, it is essential to acknowledge the connection between our minds and our bodies when it comes to emotional eating and weight management. Today we live in a hectic and packed world that is weighing us down. However, mindful meditation can be a powerful tool to help you to be able to create a rational relationship with the food that you eat. One of the essential things about overcoming emotional eating is not to avoid the emotions, but rather to face them head-on and accept them the way they are and agree that they are a crucial part of your life.

If you want to stop emotional eating, you need to be able to shift your beliefs and worthiness. You need to be able to create a means to cope with unhealthy situations. It is essential to note that meditation will not cure your emotional eating completely. Instead, it will help you examine and rationalize all the underlining sensations leading to emotional eating in your life. For emotional eaters, the feeling of guilt, shame, and low self-esteem are widespread.

These negative emotions create judgment in their minds and trigger unhealthy eating patterns, and they end up feeling like an endless self-perpetuating loop. Meditation helps you to be able to develop a non-judgmental mindset about observing your reality. That mindset will help you suppress your negative emotions feelings without even trying to suppress them or comfort them with food.

Develop the Mind, and Body connection

Meditation will help you to develop the mind and body connection. And once you're able to create that connection, you will be able to distinguish between emotional eating and physical hunger. Once you can differentiate between that, you'll be able to recognize your cues for hunger and safety. You will instantly tell when your desire is not related to physical hunger. Research indicates that medication will help to strengthen your prefrontal cortex, which is the part of the brain that helps you with willpower. That part of the brain is the part of the brain that allows us to resist the urge is within us. Mindfulness will help the calls to eat even when they're not hungry.

By strengthening that prefrontal cortex, you'll get comfortable observing those impulses without acting on them. If you want to get rid of unhealthy habits and start to build new ones, you need to be able to work on your prefrontal cortex, and you can only do that with meditation. Once you start meditating, you will begin reaping the benefits. You will learn how to be able to live more in the present. You'll become more aware of your thinking patterns, and in no time, you will be able to become conscious of how you treat food. You'll be able to make the right choice when it comes to food.

Chapter 8.   Positive Affirmations

George taught Bonnie a hundred useful positive affirmations for weight loss and to keep her motivated. She chose the ones that she wanted to build in her program and used them every day. Bonnie was losing weight very slowly, which bothered her very much. She thought she was going in the wrong direction and was about to give up, but George told her not to worry because it was a completely natural speed. It takes time for the subconscious to collate all the information and start working according to her conscious will. Besides, her body remembered the fast weight loss, but her subconscious remembered her emotional damage, and now it is trying to prevent it. In reality, after some months of hard work, she started to see the desired results. She weighed 74 kilos (163 lbs.).

According to dietitians, dieting success is greatly influenced by how people talk about lifestyle changes for others and themselves.

The use of "I should" or "I must" is to avoid whenever possible. Anyone who says, "I shouldn't eat French fries," or "I have to get a bite of chocolate" will feel that they have no control over the events. Instead, if you say "I prefer" to leave the food, you will feel more power and less guilt. The term "dieting" should be avoided. Proper nutrition is as a permanent lifestyle change. For example, the correct wording is, "I've changed my eating habits" or "I'm eating healthier."

Diets Are Fattening, Why?

The body needs fat. Our body wants to live, so it stores fat. Removing this amount of fat from the body is not easy as the body protects against weight loss. Our bodies switch to a 'saving flame' during starvation, burning fewer calories to avoid starving. Those who are starting to lose weight are usually optimistic, as, during the first week, they may experience 1-3 kg (2-7 lbs.) of weight loss, which validates their efforts and suffering. Their body, however, has deceived them very well because it actually does not want to break down fat. Instead, it begins to break down muscle tissue. At the beginning of dieting, our bodies burn sugar and protein, not fat. Burned sugar removes a lot of water out of the body; that's why we experience amazing results on the scale. It should take about seven days for our body to switch to fat burning. Then our body's alarm bell rings. Most diets have a sad end: reducing your metabolic rate to a lower level. Meaning, that if you only eat a little more afterward, you regain all the weight you have lost previously. After dieting, the body will make special efforts to store fat for the next impending famine. What to do to prevent such a situation?

We must understand what our soul needs. Those who really desire to have success must first and foremost change their spiritual foundation. It is important to pamper our souls during a period of weight loss. All overweight people tend to rag on themselves for eating forbidden food, "I overate again. My willpower is so weak!" If you have ever tried to lose weight, you know these thoughts very well.

Imagine a person very close to you who has gone through a difficult time while making mistakes from time to time. Are we going to scold or try to help and motivate them? If we really love them, we will instead comfort them and try to convince them to continue. No one tells their best friend that they are weak, ugly, or bad just because they are struggling with their weight. If you wouldn't say it to your friend, don't do so to yourself either! Let us be aware of this: during weight loss, our soul needs peace and support. Realistic thinking is more useful than disaster theory. If you are generally a healthy consumer, eat some goodies sometimes because of their delicious taste and pamper your soul.

I'll give you a list of a hundred positive affirmations you can use to reinforce your weight loss. I'll divide them into main categories based on the most typical situations for which you would need confirmation. You can repeat all of them whenever you need to, but you can also choose the more suitable ones for your circumstances. If you prefer to listen to them during meditation, you can record them with a piece of sweet relaxing music in the background.

General Affirmations to Reinforce Your Wellbeing

1. I'm grateful that I woke up today. Thank you for making me happy today.

2. Today is a perfect day. I meet nice and helpful people whom I treat kindly.

3. Every new day is for me. I live to make myself feel good. Today I just pick good thoughts for myself.

4. Something wonderful is happening to me today.

5. I feel good.

6. I am calm, energetic, and cheerful.

7. My organs are healthy.

8. I am satisfied and balanced.

9. I live in peace and understanding with everyone.

10. I listen to others with patience.

11. In every situation, I find the good.

12. I accept and respect myself and my fellow human beings.

13. I trust myself; I trust my inner wisdom.

Do you often scold yourself? Then repeat the following affirmations frequently:

14. I forgive myself.

15. I'm good to myself.

16. I motivate myself over and over again.

17. I'm doing my job well.

18. I care about myself.

19. I am doing my best.

20. I am proud of myself for my achievements.

21. I am aware that sometimes I have to pamper my soul.

22. I remember that I did a great job this week.

23. I deserved this small piece of candy.

24. I let go of the feeling of guilt.

25. I release the blame.

26. Everyone is imperfect. I accept that I am too.

If you feel pain when you choose to avoid delicious food, then you need to motivate yourself with affirmations such as:

27. I am motivated and persistent.

28. I control my life and my weight.

29. I'm ready to change my life.

30. Changes make me feel better.

31. I follow my diet with joy and cheerfulness.

32. I am aware of my amazing capacities.

33. I am grateful for my opportunities.

34. Today I'm excited to start a new diet.

35. I always keep in mind my goals.

36. I imagine myself slim and beautiful.

37. Today I am happy to have the opportunity to do what I have long been postponing.

38. I possess the energy and will to go through my diet.

39. I prefer to lose weight instead of wasting time on momentary pleasures.

Here you can find affirmations that help you to change harmful convictions and blockages:

40. I see my progress every day.

41. I listen to my body's messages.

42. I'm taking care of my health.

43. I eat healthy food.

44. I love who I am.

45. I love how life supports me.

46. A good parking space, coffee, conversation. It's all for me today.

47. It feels good to be awake because I can live in peace, health, love.

48. I'm grateful that I woke up. I take a deep breath of peace and tranquility.

49. I love my body. I love being served by me.

50. I eat by tasting every flavor of the food.

51. I am aware of the benefits of healthy food.

52. I enjoy eating healthy food and being fitter every day.

53. I feel energetic because I eat well.

Many people are struggling with being overweight because they don't move enough. The root of this issue can be a refusal to do exercises due to our minds' negative biases.

We can overcome these beliefs by repeating the following affirmations:

54. I like moving because it helps my body burn fat.

55. Each time I exercise, I am getting closer to having a beautiful, tight shapely body.

56. It's a very uplifting feeling of being able to climb up to 100 steps without stopping.

57. It's easier to have an excellent quality of life if I move.

58. I like the feeling of returning to my home tired but happy after a long winter walk.

59. Physical exercises help me have a longer life.

60. I am proud to have better fitness and agility.

61. I feel happier thanks to the happiness hormone produced by exercise.

62. I feel full thanks to the enzymes that produce a sense of fullness during physical exercises.

63. I am aware that even after exercise, my muscles continue to burn fat, so I lose weight while resting.

64. I feel more energetic after exercises.

65. My goal is to lose weight; therefore, I exercise.

66. I am motivated to exercise every day.

67. I lose weight while I exercise.

Now, I am going to give you a list of generic affirmations that you can build in your program:

68. I'm glad I'm who I am.

69. Today, I read articles and watch movies that make me feel positive about my diet progress.

70. I love it when I'm happy.

71. I take a deep breath and exhale my fears.

72. Today I do not want to prove my truth, but I want to be happy.

73. I am strong and healthy. I'm fine, and I'm getting better.

74. I am happy today because whatever I do, I find joy in it.

75. I pay attention to what I can become.

76. I love myself and am helpful to others.

77. I accept what I cannot change.

78. I am happy that I can eat healthy food.

79. I am happy that I have been changing my life with my new healthy lifestyle.

80. Today I do not compare myself to others.

81. I accept and support who I am and turn to myself with love.

82. Today I can do anything for my improvement.

83. I'm fine. I'm happy for my life. I love who I am. I'm strong and confident.

84. I am calm and satisfied.

85. Today is perfect for me to exercise and to be healthy.

86. I have decided to lose weight, and I am strong enough to follow my will.

87. I love myself, so I want to lose weight.

88. I am proud of myself because I follow my diet program.

89. I see how much stronger I am.

90. I know that I can do it.

91. It is not my past but my present that defines me.

92. I am grateful for my life.

93. I am grateful for my body because it collaborates well with me.

94. Eating healthy foods supports me in getting the best nutrients I need to be in the best shape.

95. I eat only healthy foods, and I avoid processed foods.

96. I can achieve my weight loss goals.

97. All cells in my body are fit and healthy, and so am I.

98. I enjoy staying healthy and sustaining my ideal weight.

99. I feel that my body is losing weight right now.

100. I care about my body by exercising every day.

Chapter 9.   The Power of Affirmations

Today is another day. Today is a day for you to start making a euphoric, satisfying life. Today is the day to begin to discharge every one of your impediments. Today is the day for you to get familiar with the privileged insights of life. You can transform yourself into improving things. You, as of now, include the devices inside you to do as such. These devices are your considerations and your convictions.

What Are Positive Affirmations?

For those of you who aren't acquainted with the advantages of positive affirmations, I'd prefer to clarify a little about them. A statement is genuinely anything you state or think. A great deal of what we typically report and believe is very harmful and doesn't make great encounters for us. We need to retrain our reasoning and talk into positive examples if we need to change ourselves completely.

An affirmation opens the entryway. It's a starting point on the way to change. When I talk about doing affirmations, I mean deliberately picking words that will either help take out something from your life or help make something new in your life.

Each idea you think and each word you express is an affirmation. The entirety of our self-talk, our interior exchange, is a flood of oaths. You're utilizing statements each second, whether you know it or not. You're insisting on and making your background with each word and thought.

Your convictions are just routine reasoning examples that you learned as a youngster. The vast numbers of them work very well for you. Different beliefs might be restricting your capacity to make the very things you state you need. What you need and what you trust your merit might be unusual. You have to focus on your contemplations with the goal that you can start to dispose of the ones making encounters you don't need in your life.

It would help if you understood that each grievance is an affirmation of something you figure you don't need in your life. Each time you blow up, you're asserting that you need more annoyance in your life. Each time you feel like a casualty, you're confirming that you need to keep on feeling like a casualty. If you believe that you think that life isn't giving you what you need in your reality, at that point, it's sure that you will never have the treats that experience provides for others-that is, until you change how you think and talk.

You're not a terrible individual for intuition, how you do. You've quite recently never figured out how to think and talk. Individuals all through the world are quite recently starting to discover that our contemplations make our encounters. Your folks most likely didn't have the foggiest idea about this, so they couldn't in any way, shape, or form instruct it to you. They showed you what to look like at life in the manner that their folks told them. So, no one isn't right. In any case, it's the ideal opportunity for us all to wake up and start to deliberately make our lives in a manner that satisfies and bolsters us. You can do it. I can do it. We, as a whole, can do it—we need to figure out how. So how about we get to it.

I'll talk about affirmations as a rule, and afterward, I'll get too specific to everyday issues and tell you the best way to roll out positive improvements in your well-being, funds, affection life, etc. Once you figure out how to utilize affirmations, at that point, you can apply the standards in all circumstances. A few people say that "affirmations don't work" (which is an affirmation in itself) when what they mean is that they don't have a clue how to utilize them accurately. Some of the time, individuals will say their affirmations once per day and gripe the remainder of the time. It will require some investment for affirmations to work if they're done that way. The grumbling affirmations will consistently win because there is a higher amount of them, and they're generally said with extraordinary inclination.

In any case, saying affirmations is just a piece of the procedure. What you wrap up of the day and night is significantly progressively significant. The key to having your statements work rapidly and reliably is to set up air for them to develop in. Affirmations resemble seeds planted in soil: poor soil, poor development. Fertile soil, bottomless event. The more you decide to think contemplations that cause you to feel great, the faster the affirmations work.

So, think upbeat musings; it's that straightforward. What's more, it is feasible. How you decide to believe, at this point, is just that, a decision. You may not understand it since you've thought along these lines for such a long time, yet it truly is a decision. Presently, today, this second, you can decide to change your reasoning. Your life won't pivot for the time being. Yet, in case you're reliable and settle on the decision regularly to think about considerations that cause you to feel great, you'll unquestionably roll out positive improvements in each part of your life.

Positive Affirmations and How to Use Them

Positive affirmations are positive articulations that depict an ideal circumstance, propensity, or objective that you need to accomplish. Rehashing regularly these positive explanations influences the psyche brain profoundly, and triggers it without hesitation, to bring what you are reworking into the real world.

The demonstration of rehashing the affirmations, intellectually or so anyone might hear, inspires the individual reworking them, builds the desire and inspiration, and pulls in open doors for development and achievement.

Likewise, this demonstration programs the psyche to act as per the rehashed words, setting off the inner mind-brain to take a shot at one's sake, to offer the positive expressions materialize.

Affirmations are extremely valuable for building new propensities, rolling out positive improvements throughout one's life, and accomplishing objectives. Affirmations help in weight misfortune, getting progressively engaged, concentrating better, changing propensities, and achieving dreams. They can be helpful in sports, in business, improving one's wellbeing, weight training, and in numerous different zones.

These positive articulations influence in a proper manner the body, the brain, and one's sentiments. Rehashing affirmations is very reasonable. Despite this, a lot of people do not know about this truth. Individuals, for the most part, restate negative statements, not positive ones. This is called negative self-talk.

In the event that you've been revealing to yourself that you can't contemplate how miserable you are, that you need more money, or how troublesome life is, you've been repeating negative affirmations.

In this sense, you make more challenges and issues since you are concentrating on the problems, and in this way, expanding them, rather than concentrating on the arrangements.

Many people rehash in their psyches pessimistic words and proclamations concerning the contrary circumstances and occasions in their lives, and therefore, make progressively bothersome circumstances.

Words work in two different ways, to assemble or obliterate. It is how we use them that decides if they will bring tremendous or destructive outcomes.

Affirmations in Modern Times

It is said that the French analyst and drug specialist Emile Coue is the individual who carried this subject to the open's consideration in the mid-twentieth century.

Emile Coue saw that when he told his patients how viable an elixir was, the outcomes were superior to if he didn't utter a word. He understood that musings that consume our psyches become a reality and that rehashing concepts and considerations is a sort of autosuggestion.

Emile Coue is associated with his acclaimed proclamation, "*Consistently, all around, I am showing signs of improvement and better.*"

Later in the twentieth century, Louise Hay was concentrated on this point and called autosuggestions—affirmations.

Chapter 10.   Weight Loss Affirmations

Affirmations are verbal statements that help us to affirm something we believe. So often, we say negative affirmations to ourselves without even realizing it. Recognize those negative thoughts and replace them with the positive statement that we have listed below. Repeat these to yourself daily. Write them down on a piece of paper or have notes on them that you leave throughout your house. Remember to practice your breathing exercises that we have learned through the other mindset exercises, and keep an open mind as always.

Affirmations to Lose Weight Naturally

Losing weight is more than just looking good to me. I understand that I need to live a healthy lifestyle to feel better all of the time.

I know how to lose weight, and actually, I choose to do this naturally because it helps me be healthier. I know what I need to do to get the things I deserve from this life.

I am capable of reaching all of the goals that I set for myself, and I am the one who decides what I do next with my life.

I recognize that it's essential for me to be patient throughout this process. I can wait for the results because I know that I will get everything that I want in the end. I do not punish myself because I don't achieve a goal as fast as I initially hoped. I nourish myself throughout this process. I continuously look for ways to encourage myself and build my self-esteem because I know that will help me feel the best in the end. I can control my impulses. I know how not to act on my highest urges. I recognize the methods that will help me to enable myself to work harder in the end. I am happy because I know how to say no.

I can turn away when I'm confronted with an impulse. I am more durable than the biggest cravings that I have. I am proud of my ability to have a high level of willpower. I trust myself around certain foods and recognize that what tempts me does not control me.

I look at the things that I already have in my life instead of only paying attention to something that I don't have.

This is the way that will help me better achieve everything that I desire. I do not allow distractions to keep me from getting the things that I want. I can stay focused on my goals so that I can create the life that I deserve. In the end, even when I am tempted by something or somebody else, I know how to push through this urge and instead focus on my goals. I will wait for everything. Love is coming to me because I know that, when it does, I will feel entirely fulfilled. I am enjoying the journey and the process that it takes to get the body that I want. I recognize that small milestones are worth celebrating.

I do not wait for one big goal to be reached to be happy with myself. I look for all the methods needed to achieve greatness in this life. I understand that a temporary desire to eat something unhealthy is not worth giving up on all of my goals. I know how to distract myself from my biggest cravings so that I can do something healthy instead. I recognize that doing something small is better than doing nothing at all. Even on the days that I don't want to go to the gym, I do something at home to work out so that I can at least accomplish something minor.

Just getting started is the hardest part for me, but I know how to work through those feelings now. I am emotionally aware of what might be holding me back, not to allow myself to tempt me by distractions.

I control my feelings and my urges so that I don't do anything that I regret. I am happy because I am knowledgeable about the things that make me who I am.

I forgive myself when I do act on an impulse. I don't punish myself or deprive my body of the first things that it needs just because I did something wrong. I sacrifice certain things that I want but never to a point where I cause punishment or torture on myself. I am successful because I am dedicated. I have strong willpower because I am successful. I move through my life with gratitude and always appreciate the things that I have around me. I can pick myself up when I'm feeling weak.

I appreciate even the hard parts of my life because they create the person I am. I am a talented and influential person. I have control over my body, and nobody else does. I recognize my weaknesses, but in the same breath, I am very aware of my strengths. I balance my life with these things. I empower my strengths and thrive when I am in an environment that helps me grow. I recognize my weaknesses, and I always look for ways to turn them around to live more happily and healthily after. I cook meals for myself because it makes me feel healthier and more reliable in the end.

I am going to get the dream body that I want because I can recognize things that might be healthy or unhealthy for me. I move my body at least once a day. I always feel better after I agree to a workout rather than if I try to avoid one. I can give myself rest when I need it. I don't push myself when I'm too stressed out because I know that this isn't going to help me get the things that I want.

I can always find motivation and passion within myself. I set my own goals, and I set newer and bigger ones after I achieved ones that I already completed. I do not procrastinate with my goals. I know what I have to do every single day to reach these goals, and I always look for ways to go above and beyond as well. I am continually improving the methods that I use to live a healthy lifestyle. I self-reflect so that I can find real solutions to any issues that I might face. I don't let what other people think to take over how I see myself. I am not afraid of judgment from other people because I know that not everything negative that somebody thinks about me is right.

I make the right decision for my body. I understand that even if I make wrong decisions, sometimes, they all play a vital role in making me the person that I am today. These struggles are something that I had to undergo to become the powerful individual that I am.

I am continually losing weight because of all this dedication and passion. I feel lighter, happier, and healthier. I am free. I am pure and clean. I am collected and calm. I am peaceful, and I am so glad. I heal myself through my weight loss. I take everything wrong that I did to my body in the past and turn it into something useful as I exercise and make healthy choices. I am always getting closer and closer to the things that I want. I'm focused on pushing through my most significant setbacks to achieve the things that I deserve. I do not sit around and fantasize about what I want anymore. Instead, I know exactly how to get this. I believe in myself because I know that this is going to be an essential part of my journey. I trust my ability to lose weight, and I'm not afraid of what will happen if I don't. I know how to say these affirmations to myself when I feel better.

Other people like being around me. Others recognize my hard work. Others know that I deserve to have good things in my life. When I listened to my body, I can thrive. I recognize the things that my body tells me to get the best results possible.

I feel good, and I look even better. I look great, and I look incredible because of this. Not only does losing weight help my body look better, but it also helps my soul, which can show through so quickly to other people. I choose to do things that are good for my body. I value myself, and I have virtue in all that I do. I add value to other people's lives, as well. I motivate myself, and therefore, I know how to motivate other people.

I am not afraid of anything. The worst thing that can happen to me is that I stop believing in myself. I will always be my best friend. I will still know how to encourage myself and include confidence in everything that I do. I love myself, and I am proud of the body that I have. I am perfect the way that I am, and I am beautiful. I am happy I am healthy, and I am free. I am focused, I am centered, and I am peaceful. I am stress-free and thankful. I have gratitude and love. I am attractive, and I am perfect. There is nothing that I need to punish myself for.

Chapter 11.   Losing Weight with Hypnosis: A Real Replacement for Diet

It is not a magical method, and we must have it clear; it will not allow us to lose weight immediately, but it is a tool that will help us to adopt correct habits regarding food.

It is also essential that it is clear that this method can work for some people, not others, since some are more receptive than others and do not have any side effects. Hence there are opinions against hypnosis.

The entire process or treatment is one month, and usually with sessions of two hours a week.

The fields covered by hypnosis are many. This helps us to overcome emotionally stress, phobias, or the entire universe that our mind thinks is a problem, in addition to anesthesia, to lose weight. It is also attractive clinical hypnosis to treat the issues of smoking and alcoholism, among others.

Goodbye diet and the yo-yo effect, Hello wish Figure: hypnotherapy, the body is healthy to lose weight, it helps to maintain the bodyweight of a long-term hope—the stomach and food desire to put out a growl. Is this idea too good? Show what is behind the extraordinary weight loss methods and see if it turns the pounds effortlessly.

Give up carbohydrates and count calorie and juice treatments rigorously instead of feasting. Many women try countless diets and seemingly healthy diet changes to lose weight quickly. However, if a terrible yo-yo effect occurs after the end of the hunger customer diet, there will soon be no exhilaration of short-term customer impact. In theory, it sounds straightforward.

The key to a slim and healthy body is conscious and balanced nutrition and adequate exercise. The switch from "Sports Muffle" to "Fitness Guru" is chocolate and fast food. It is easier than merely replacing it with fruits and vegetables.

Can your head switch regularly interfere with your diet plan? With the help of hypnosis therapy? My editorial staff investigates what is behind the promise to relieve stress-free with hypnosis and reveals whether a mental strategy against excess pounds is promising.

Is it possible?

Hypnosis: is that real, or is it just a promise of the sky?

Weight Loss Due to Hypnosis

Weight loss due to hypnosis-sounds like a dream for Martina S. She already had a long diet odyssey behind her. She failed with FdH, combined meals, dieted, and slimmed drinks. After she finally approached her ideal weight with Weight Watchers, the pound returned to her waist after the program.

Then she read a daily newspaper ad: "*Hypnotizing to the desired weight-simple, permanent, without* willpower *and meals.*" Then she got new hope. With a price of 100 euros in a one-off session and a promised success rate of 80%, we dare to make a relatively realistic female attempt in other respects. In a few days, 12 overweight people practice advertising on a beach located in Schleswig-Holstein. "I was relatively excited before, but this session had nothing to do with the Hypnose Hype show on TV."

Like snoozing in the sun.

"Since then, the actual transformer treatment has begun," the nurse says. During hypnosis, she felt as relaxed as when she fell asleep in the sun. *"In the distance, I heard the therapist say that I will eat when I am hungry.* Martina says, *"I will not eat after 6 pm."* Today, three months later, a scale is about 15 kilometers less, and Martina's desire for sweets is not overwhelming. *"It's almost scary, but there is no desire for chocolate or fatty food. Even colleagues have already realized that they can't even reach their nostrils automatically."* Work?

Example of a Case of Weight Loss by Hypnosis

An overweight woman asked me for help in controlling her diet. His problem was a compulsion to eat popcorn. She bought them in packages of 45 kg, ate popcorn with butter at all hours, and quench his thirst; she drank copious amounts of soda. Butter, salt, and soda were more harmful to her than popcorn, although they represented the vehicle for ingesting the other products. So it was appropriate to make popcorn, not to your liking.

Before I hypnotized her, I tried to discover what foods she didn't like, but she seemed to like everything.

"Is there nothing that you find repulsive?" I asked on the edge of despair.

"Well, yes," she replied. «The wet feathers of chickens make me sick. I can't stand its smell. My father forced me to kill and peel chickens against my will.» I had finally found something she didn't like. When we practiced the exercise, we reached the moment when she should put something in her mouth; I said, "There is a large bowl full of popcorn in front of you, but they have been in contact with wet chicken feathers. Popcorn smells like feathers. Now take a handful of popcorn and place it in your mouth. She immediately began to gag and feel nauseous. I thought she was about to throw up.

When she left the office and arrived at his house, she prepared some popcorn. It was then that she vomited. Every day she tried to eat popcorn, but the mere fact of preparing them made her nauseous. When she returned to the office for the third session, she was not even trying to develop the popcorn; she had abandoned the habit and was losing weight. When she stopped eating popcorn, she also left soda, butter, and salt.

When we were approaching session number 6, she had already lost almost 9 kilos and felt very good. I told her to add more fruit and vegetables to the diet. She had stopped being a popcorn addict.

The lesson we must learn from this example is that it is necessary to discover some taste or smell repulsive to the patient. Such flavors or odors will be used later to eliminate harmful habits. Most often, the problem is sweets, such as chocolate or cakes. Suppose the subject drinks 51 pounds (2 kilos) of chocolate a day and hates the taste of the liver. In that case, he should instruct to visualize himself removing a piece of chocolate from the fridge that has been very close to a part of 2 kilos of the fresh liver. The taste and smell of the liver have permeated chocolate; you can get an idea.

Exercises before Hypnosis

Below, I will present two exercises before hypnosis. You must use them during the consultation period to become familiar with hypnosis and to feel comfortable. Words written in italics indicate the text that should be said aloud.

Exercise 1

I want you to close your eyes for a short workout. I want you to imagine a blackboard, to believe it. It can be black or green, or the color you want. Believe it, the board has a tray, and there are chalk and an eraser on it. Do you see it?

(Wait for the answer. When the subject answers affirmatively, you can continue.)

Very well. Now take chalk and draw a circle on the board. Have you brought it yet?

Good. Now write the letter A inside the circle. Have you done it yet?

Now you delete the letter A inside the circle but do not remove the ring. Let me know when you're done.

(Wait for the answer).

Very good. Now erase the circle and open your eyes.

At this point, you can briefly talk with the patient about the experience of the board. Assure him that whatever knowledge he has had, has been positive. Each person responds differently. Some see the board. Others intuit it. Some know that it is there. All the answers are correct. In hypnosis, there are no erroneous experiences. Each person lives the situations in a personal way, and all the skills are valid. Clarify to the patient that these types of responses are frequent in hypnosis.

Exercise 2

Close your eyes once again to perform another training exercise. This time I want him to focus his attention on the tip of his nose. Has it done?

Wait for the affirmative answer, and continue.

All right. Keep your attention on the tip of the nose and listen to my voice's sound in some of the hypnosis techniques that we will do together. If you warn that your mind wanders at any time during hypnosis, all you have to do is focus again on the tip of your nose, just as you are doing right now. Then your account will stop wavering and concentrate on my voice again. Now you can open your eyes.

Chapter 12.   Why Is It Hard to Lose Weight?

For anyone who has ever struggled with weight, life can seem like an uphill battle. It can be downright devastating to see how difficult it can be to turn things around and shed some weight.

The fact of the matter is that losing weight doesn't have to be an uphill battle. Most of this requires you to understand better why this struggle happens and what you can do to help give yourself a fighting chance.

Physiological factors are affecting your ability to lose weight. There are also psychological, emotional and even spiritual causes that affect your overall body's ability to help you lose weight and reach your ideal weight levels.

The Obvious Culprits

The obvious culprits that are holding you back are diet, a lack of exercise and a combination of both.

First off, your diet plays a crucial role in your overall health and wellbeing. When it comes to weight management, your diet has everything to do with your ability to stay in shape and ward of unwanted weight.

When it comes to diet, we are not talking about keto, vegan, or Atkins; we are talking about the common foods you consume and the amounts you have of each one, which is why diet is one of the obvious culprits. If you have a diet that is high in fat, high in sodium and high in sugar, you can rest assured that your body will end up gaining weight at a rapid rate.

When you consume high amounts of sugar, carbs, and fats, your body transforms them into glucose, storing them in the body as fat. Of course, a proportion of the glucose produced by your body is used up as energy. However, if you consume far more than you need, your body isn't going to get rid of it; your body is going to hold on to it and make sure that it is stored for a rainy day.

Here is another vital aspect to consider: sweet and salty foods, the kind that we love so dearly, trigger "happy hormones" in the brain, namely dopamine. Dopamine is a hormone that is released by the body when it "feels good." And the food is one of the best ways to trigger it, which is why you somehow feel better after eating your favorite meals. It also explains the reason why we resort to food when we are not feeling well which is called "comfort food," and it is one of the most popular coping mechanisms employed by folks around the world.

This rush of dopamine causes a person to become addicted to food. As with any addiction, there comes a time when you need to get more and more of that same substances to meet your body's requirements.

As a result of diet, a lack of regular exercise can do a number on your ability to lose weight and maintain a healthy balance. What regular exercise does is increase your body's overall caloric requirement. As such, your metabolism needs to convert fat at higher rates to keep up with your body's energy demands.

As the body's energetic requirements increase, that is, as your exercise regimen gets more and more intense, you will find that you will need increased amounts of both oxygen and glucose, which is one of the reasons why you feel hungrier when you ramp up your workouts.

However, increased caloric intake isn't just about consuming more and more calories for the sake of consuming more and more calories; you need to consume an equal amount of proteins, carbs, fats and vitamins too for your body to build the necessary elements that will build muscle, foster movement and provide proper oxygenation in the blood.

Moreover, nutrients are required for the body to recover. One of the byproducts of exercise is called "lactic acid." Lactic acid builds up in the muscles as they get more and more tired. Lactic acid signals the body that it is time to stop working out or risk injury if you continue. Without lactic acid, your body would have no way of knowing when your muscles have overextended their capacity.

After you have completed your workout, the body needs to get rid of the lactic acid buildup. So, if you don't have enough of the right minerals in your body, for example, potassium, your muscles will ache for days until your body is finally able to get rid of the lactic acid buildup. This example shows how proper nutrition is needed to help the body get moving and recover once it is done exercising.

As a result, a lack of exercise reconfigures your body's metabolism to work at a slower pace. What that means is that you need to consume fewer calories to fuel your body's lack of exercise. So, if you end up wasting more than you need, your body will just put it away for a rainy day. Plain and simple.

The Sneaky Culprits

The sneaky culprits are the ones that aren't quite so overt in causing you to gain weight or have trouble shedding pounds. These culprits hide beneath the surface but are very useful when it comes to keeping you overweight. The first culprit we are going to be looking at is called "stress."

Stress is a potent force. From an evolutionary perspective, it exists as a means of fueling the flight-or-fight response. Stress is the human response to danger. When a person senses danger, the body begins to secrete a hormone called "cortisol." When cortisol begins running through the body, it signals the entire system to prep for a potential showdown. Depending on the situation, it might be best to hightail it out and live to fight another day.

In our modern way of life, stress isn't so much a response to life and death situations (though it can certainly be). Instead, it is the response to cases that are deemed as "conflictive" by the mind. This could be a confrontation with a co-worker, bumper-to-bumper traffic, or any other type of situation in which a person feels vulnerable in some way.

Throughout our lives, we subject to countless interactions in which we must deal with stress. In general terms, the feelings of alertness subside when the perceived threat is gone. However, when a person is exposed to prolonged periods of stress, any number of changes can happen.

One such change is overexposure to cortisol. When there is too much cortisol in the body, the body's overall response is to hoard calories, increase the production of other hormones such as adrenaline and kick up the immune system's function.

This response by the body is akin to the panic response that the body would assume when faced with prolonged periods of hunger or fasting. As a result, the body needs to go into survival mode. Please bear in mind that the body has no clue if it is being chased by a bear, dealing with a natural disaster or just having a bad day at the office. Regardless of the circumstances, the body is faced with the need to ensure its survival. So, anything that it eats goes straight to fat stores.

Moreover, a person's stressful situation makes them search for comfort and solace. There are various means of achieving this. Food is one of them. So is alcohol consumption. These two types of pleasures lead to significant use of calories. Again, when the body is in high gear, it will store as many calories and keep them in reserve. This is what makes you gain weight when you are stressed out.

Another of the sneaky culprits is sleep deprivation. In short, sleep deprivation is sleeping less than the recommended 8 hours that all adults should sleep. In children's cases, the recommended amount of sleep can be anywhere from 8 to 12 hours, depending on their age.

Granted, some adults can function perfectly well with less than 8 hours' sleep. Some folks can work perfectly well with 6 hours' sleep, while there are folks who are shattered when they don't get eight or even more hours of sleep. This is different for everyone as each individual is different in this regard.

That being said, sleep deprivation can trigger massive amounts of cortisol. This, fueled by ongoing exposure to stress, leads the body to further deepening its panic mode. When this occurs, you can rest assured that striking a healthy balance between emotional wellbeing and physical health can be nearly impossible to achieve.

Now, the best way to overcome sleep deprivation is to get sleep, but that is easier said than done. One of the best ways to get back on track to a certain degree is to get in enough sleep when you can.

The last sneaky culprit on our list is emotional distress. Emotional distress can occur as a result of any number of factors. For example, the loss of a loved one, a stressful move, a divorce, or the loss of a job can contribute to large amounts of emotional distress. While all of the situations mentioned above begin as stressful situations, they can fester and lead to severe psychological issues. Over time, these emotional issues can grow into more profound topics such as General Anxiety Disorder or Depression. Studies have shown that prolonged periods of stress can lead to depression and a condition known as Major Depression.

The most common course of treatment for anxiety and depression is the use of an antidepressant. And, guess what: one of the side effects associated with antidepressants is gain weight. The reason for this is that antidepressants tinker with the brain's chemistry in such a way that they alter the brain's processing of chemicals through the suppression of serotonin transport. This causes the brain to readjust its overall chemistry. Thus, you might find the body unable to process food quite the same way. In general, it is common to see folks gain as much as 10 pounds as a result of taking antidepressants.

As you can see, weight gain is not the result of "laziness" or being "undisciplined." Sure, you might have to clean up your diet somewhat and get more exercise. But the causes we have outlined here ought to provide you with enough material to see why there are less obvious causes that are keeping yours from achieving your ideal weight. This is why meditation plays such a key role in helping you deal with stress and emotional strife while helping you find a balance between your overall mental and physical wellbeing.

Ultimately, the strategies and techniques that we will further outline here will provide you with the tools that will help you strike that balance and eventually lead you to find the most effective way in which you will deal with the rigors of your day-to-day life while being able to make the most out of your efforts to lead a healthier life. You have everything you need to do it. So, let's find out how you can achieve this.

Chapter 13.   Background Information for Weight Loss

Understand Your Habits

You may find yourself developing some habits without knowing. The same applies to create excellent health practice. Your daily practices and choices explain your current conditions. Stop complaining; do focus on your habits and remember, your preferences will define who you will be. Albert Einstein goes on to say, *"we cannot solve our problems with the same thinking we used when we created them."* Step out of your bubble a given structure for the desired outcome. Really the hardest part is starting, and you've already done that, and it will only get more accessible and more natural, the more you participate, and the more you take an active role in this journey.

Consider habits development as elaborated in the story of a miller and a camel on a winter's day. It was freezing outside, and while the miller slept, he was awakened by a noise at the door. When he opened his eyes, he heard a camel's voice complaining that it was cold outside and asking to warm his nose inside. Miller agreed that all he had to do was insert the mouthpiece. A little later, the camel put on his forehead, then his neck, then other parts of his body, then his whole body little by little until he started destroying things inside the house. He started walking around the house, tripping over anything in his path. When the miller ordered the camel to leave, the camel boasted that he was comfortable inside and would not leave. The camel went further and told the miller that he could leave whenever he wanted. The same thing happens with a habit that comes all at once and takes hold of you.

Maybe you started out smoking your first cigarette, thinking it was disgusting, and then years go by, and you have a nasty habit. Well, bad habits can sneak in, but the same philosophy can apply to ethical practices. Just take it bit-by-bit and step-by-step, and before you know it, you have healthy habits in your life. There are so many challenges to healthy eating. You have to be willing to have an open mind and reset your thinking on food.

It is cheaper to develop new habits; effort is the primary requirement, but not that much. When you have trained yourself new patterns, train on it every day for some time, after which it will be automatic.

We can relate that situation to a football club Coash who engages in various rigorous training with his players while awaiting the actual match. They practice new skills and moves. When match day arrives, the coach sits with the substitutes while watching the players playing from the line. Players play as per the learned skills and moves. Apply the required effort to actualize your goal.

While telling stories with your workmates, tell them how you drink 3 to 4 glasses of water every day, the same as tea. That looks strict. At heart, you know how your consumption of water and team is reduced while at home. This is self-discipline. Self-discipline calls for the establishment of strong foundations. Efforts adopted are less.

Apply Core Solutions

Recognize and face the challenges of healthy eating and develop new habits. Like a logger trying to clear a log, identify the critical side of each situation. The well-experienced logger will try to identify essential joints by climbing up then do the clearing. A less experienced logger would start by the edge. Both methods produce expected results, but one way saves more time and uses less energy than the other. All our problems have strategic points. How about when we identify critical logs to healthy eating and offer some solutions? First, log jam. How were you brought up? You may have been forced as a child to eat vegetables and see them as something undesirable, and you built a perception that plants don't taste good. Another log jam is stress—so much pressure.

We live in a world full of pressure where time matters in all our undertakings, troubled life, and our bodies pay most of the price. You have many choices to pick from. If you are a lover of fast food, you need to stop. Fast foods are addictive, and we highly depend on them due to the positive attitude we have towards them. We are obsessed with them such that we cannot live a day without consuming them. When you eat something wrong for you, and you say you don't care. Your thoughts and focus are totally on how delicious and enjoyable it is to be eating the food that you're eating, regardless of how unhealthy it is, and then you have guilt about how those pounds are going on rather than coming off.

Such thoughts occur even when taking tasty food. We may find ourselves eating some food which in reality we know are very dangerous to our health. Chip is a prime example. An individual from a diet class may feel hungry on her way back home and decide to a branch by a fast food joint for some chips plates. Despite several cautions on the dangers of chips from class lessons, she chooses to eat chips—what a radical idea. Most people have mental disorders making it difficult to stop taking some food even though we understand their bodies' repercussions, i.e. eating chips. An article on this topic claims that most food companies are working hard at night to make fast food more addictive. According to Howard Moskovitz, a consultant in the junk food industry, they put more flavor on junk food to make you come back for more. If the food tastes too good, then we'd have what's called a sensory-specific Satia T, then we wouldn't want anymore. So, companies have to find just the right balance of flavors. So, there's not too much or too little. All they do is balance the flavors. That balance is called Bliss point.

According to Steven Weatherly, an expert in junk food, Cheetos are the core source of pleasure. They are the specific type of food manufactured by big companies to satisfy you solely and not add any health benefit to your body. They are designed in such a manner that when you start eating them, it melts on your mouth, making it feels tasty and impressive. They are made to make you go for more. A friend was once a diet, and her boyfriend brought home Cheetos. Yes, she said no. She ended up just having one, and before she knew it, she ate almost the whole thing. We understand why the next log in our way we may think we don't like healthy food. Perhaps you don't like healthy food. You want foods that excite your palate to feel alive, be closer to something exciting, but you will not be satisfied.

You'll not reach the maximum point, and perhaps you will not know what to do. Normalizing bad habits make us feel comfortable in our negative thoughts. When you do one negative thing, the effects widely spread. Self-indulgence keeps us wrapped up in this safe place and keeps us inside ourselves and absorbed by negative thoughts. You know you do one thing poorly or negatively; it trickles into other areas. It leaves you feeling bad, and you do short to feel better just for the short term, such as impossible diets that you can't keep up with, and then you, you feel worse and worse about yourself and you, you go overboard when you can't keep up. It's a vicious cycle. The primary method of overcoming these key logs is first to hit the reset button. It might not be easy; strive as much as you can by having an open mind and a positive attitude in the future.

Explore various flavors even if you don't like them. Michael's sister has a negative attitude towards blueberries. She had not consumed any since her childhood and kept telling stories that had no connection to the blueberries' taste. One day Michael made her taste the blueberry, and she loved it. Test your assumptions, test your opinions because you don't know where they came from; such an assumption may be baseless. Despite her premise on blueberries being messy, and she made a try, and she ended up loving it. Open your mind to new ideas. Remember the coy's story and to keep figuratively throwing yourself into more environments meaningful to you, you will stretch and grow in size. Adopt an attitude of success, stop fetus thinking, and know that your thoughts, perceptions, and behaviors can change. Why not start to look forward to fruits and vegetables, however crazy they sound? You were not born with the thoughts you possess today; they are a construct of your mind. They can be challenged.

The next solution calls for changing one's health. Saying a big NO and breaking a cycle is all you need—cutting out indulgence.

Commit yourself daily, and you'll find it easier to overcome the notion of food industries that want you to be addicted to their food. The third is growth towards what you want and the freedom you desire. This step calls for exceptional consistency. Make your bold step a pattern. This pattern will develop into the desired habit. Unpack your true self through spiritual faith and meditative silence. Strive to become better. Look inside, stop looking for solutions on the outside. Make additional efforts like being more helpful, joyful, and caring for those who are needy, consistently reach for truth, grace, and peace in your day. Take caution on being a man of the people, and you may be living a fishy life. Finally, systems generate autonomy. We are going to be creating a system together by planning, keeping it simple, embracing balance in your life, and accomplishing these solutions and your goals by following the system to help you prioritize and reinforce consistency in your life.

The best solution to weight loss is a healthy diet and an active body. There could be a reason why doing these two is a problem from your side. The pathway will make the process more holistic and more fun. All may not be your answer, but you must get something from it.

Chapter 14.   Weight Loss Psychology

It is possible that they become exhausted or disappointed with their pace of weight loss, or endure a flashing omission and become overwhelmed by guilt, or feel excessively "denied" to proceed. And after that, trying to clarify failure, a considerable lot of them accuse their diet-plan, their residential circumstance, or their innate powerlessness to lose weight. This procedure frequently rehashes itself. As a result, a few dieters can go through years fruitlessly attempting to lose weight while never understanding the genuine reason for their difficulty. Here are three underlying mental problems we experience when trying to lose weight, alongside specific tips for how to defeat them:

Problem 1. Not Knowing How Weight Loss Will Benefit You

Regardless of whether we need to lose 20 or 220 pounds, we need to change our eating habits and maybe a few other lifestyle habits. Rolling out these improvements may not be difficult on Day 1 of Week 1 of our weight loss diet because our underlying eagerness, more often than not, gives us adequate inspiration. Generally, within 2–3 weeks, our "new" eating example begins to meddle with our standard lifestyle, and, except if we set up for this, our craving to keep dieting will start to blur. Rather than considering to be an international ID to a superior weight and shape, we believe it to be a snag and a burden. It progresses toward becoming something we are doing because we "must" instead of "need to." This is the principal enormous, passionate problem we experience when dieting.

To conquer this problem, we need to know precisely why we are attempting to lose weight. We need an unmistakable thought of how it will benefit us. If we have an obvious benefit to anticipate, will we have the option to oppose the impulse to return to our past negative behavior patterns? General benefits from having a more slender, lighter shape aren't ground-breaking enough. We need a narrow-minded, specific interest—something we can imagine—that directs our consideration. Whatever we pick, it must make a clamor inside our head! Keep in mind, the minute we begin to feel that we "need to" accomplish something, it turns into the adversary—like settling regulatory obligations or wiping out the storm cellar—and our inspiration flies out the window. To accomplish enduring weight loss, we need to "need it."

Problem 2. Attempting to Be Perfect

During my hypnotherapist experience, I've met maybe 100 dieters face to face and discuss by and by with another 1,000 over the Internet. Be that as it may, so far, I haven't met one single fruitful dieter who was immaculate. In actuality, the more significant part of my active customers committed vast amounts of errors. They had terrible days, awful weeks—even entire months—during which they went totally off the rails. In any case, none of this prevented them from prevailing at last. Why not? Since they learned from their mistakes, also, how about we do not overlook: the vast majority of our self-information originates from the mistakes we make, not our triumphs.

Tragically, numerous dieters demand to attempt to be immaculate. As a result, when they do tumble off the wagon (as they generally do), they find it difficult to endure their "failure" and become overwhelmed by guilt. So although their pass may have been generally inconsequential (a weekend gorge), they turn out badly since the blame does genuine harm, not the gorging.

The exercise is this. When dieting, don't sit around idly attempting to be impeccable. It just prompts expanded guilt and failure. Instead, please acknowledge that you are going to make mistakes and don't give them a chance to divert you when they occur. Consider them to be a learning experience. For instance, if you drink a lot of liquor when eating out and enormously gorge, as a result, don't get up the following morning in an attack of gloom. Instead, relish your experience, and welcome that you have made a necessary disclosure: that an excessive amount of liquor makes weight loss increasingly difficult. By responding this way, you will maintain a strategic distance from guilt and find it a lot simpler to come back to your diet.

Problem 3. Treating Your Diet as Race

Another regular problem concerns the speed of weight reduction. Numerous dieters hope to lose weight exceptionally quickly and are mentally ill-equipped when their bodies do not carry on in this style. If a week goes by with no weight reduction, they become disheartened and begin to lose interest. In this way, it has no enthusiasm for shedding muscle versus fat, which it sees as a significant wellspring of vitality during times of starvation.

To beat your anxiety and keep up enduring weight loss, quit thinking about your diet as a race. This decreases tension and gives you progressively "breathing space" to settle into your new eating habits. I clarify this in more detail on my excellent weight-loss discussion, and a great many people find it a gainful methodology. Simultaneously, abstain from hopping on your bathroom scales each day—confine yourself to once every week. Checking your weight more regularly urges you to take a transient perspective on things, which isn't useful.

I understand that "relentless" weight loss may not sound frightfully appealing, yet in my experience, the slower the weight loss, the more it stays off. Besides, as expressed above, if you lose multiple pounds a week, it won't be fat—it will be muscle or water and keeping in mind that losing water is just transitory—and consequently silly—losing muscle will slow your digestion and increment the danger of future weight gain.

It appears everybody nowadays is attempting to lose weight. Each time you get a magazine, turn on the TV or check out yourself, you are reminded of it. You start to hate your body, losing control, disappointed, focused on, apprehensive, and now and again even discouraged.

If losing weight is tied in with eating fewer calories than your body needs and doing some activity to support your digestion, at that point, why are such a significant number of individuals as yet attempting to lose weight?

Losing weight has to do with your considerations and convictions as much as it has to do with what you eat. Give me a chance to give you a model. You are staring at the TV, and an advertisement is shown demonstrating a chocolate cheddar cake that you can make utilizing just three fixings. You weren't hungry previously; however, since you have seen that cheddar cake, you might feel denied, and you need to eat. Your feelings are revealing to you that you have to eat, although your stomach isn't disclosing to you that you are hungry.

This is called emotional eating. It is our feelings that trigger our practices.

You may find that you have this need to eat something when you are feeling focused or depressed since it solaces you somehow or another. The issue is that generally, it isn't healthy that you get for, and once you have done this a couple of times, it turns into a passionate stay, so every time that you experience pressure or grief, it triggers you to eat something.

Grapples keep you attached to convictions that you have about your life and yourself that prevent you from pushing ahead. You regularly compensate yourself with things that prevent you from losing weight. When you're utilizing nourishment to reward or repay yourself, you are managing stays.

Although the grapples that I am alluding to around passionate eating are not healthy ones, they can likewise be utilized intentionally to get a specific outcome.

Enthusiastic eating doesn't happen because you are physically hungry. It occurs because something triggers a craving for nourishment. You are either intuitively or deliberately covering a hidden, enthusiastic need.

The fear of eating can assume control over your life. It expends your musings, depleting you of your vitality and self-discipline, making you separate and gorge. This will create more fear and make matters more regrettable.

So how might you conquer your fear and different feelings around eating?

You can transform the majority of your feelings around eating into another more beneficial relationship.

In all actuality, you have a soul. You should find it. It is that spot inside of you that is continually cherishing, forgiving and tranquil. It's a spot that speaks to your higher self... The genuine you, the sheltered, loved and entire you. When you find this, the resentment, dissatisfaction, and stress that you are feeling about your weight will vanish.

Things never appear to happen as fast as we might want them to. Perhaps your body isn't changing as quickly as you need. This may demoralize you, giving you further reason to indulge.

Comprehend that your body is a gift, and afterwards, you will begin to contemplate it.

Quit harping on your stomach fat, your fat arms and butt, your enormous thighs that you hate and every one of the calories that you're taking in, and see all that your body is, all that your body can do and all that your body is doing right now.

This new mindfulness will make love and acknowledgement for your body such that you never had. You start to treasure it like the astounding gift that it is and centre around, giving it wellbeing every day in each moment with each breath.

Begin concentrating on picking up wellbeing as opposed to losing weight, and you will be progressively happy, alive, and thankful. Find the delight of carrying on with a healthy life and feeding your soul consistently. Develop more love increasingly with your body and yourself, and this love will move and transform you from the inside out.

Chapter 15. Guided Hypnosis for Weight Loss

Even if hypnosis has no physical side effects, it has to be done well and by a certified hypnotist for it to be effective. There are many hypnotists in the market, but getting the right one is a challenge. We shall also discuss various apps that use hypnosis to aid in weight loss as well as a guide to losing weight through hypnotherapy.

Choosing a Hypnotherapist for Weight Loss

Expanding open, GP, and NHS acknowledgement of necessary treatments and hypnotherapy has explicitly brought about a gigantic increment in the number of individuals offering to prepare. The nature of this preparation fluctuates incredibly, so it is the BSCH's main goal to give its specialists an abnormal state of making and moral practice.

There are various things you are encouraged to search for when looking for a trance inducer to assist you with a specific issue:

- Where was the preparation for them?

- Have they passed an independent audit?

- Do you have literary validity in your training?

- Is there a continuous preparing framework or a CPD framework?

- Is there a supervisory framework?

- Do they have protection for expert remuneration?

- Do they pursue a composed morals code?

- Is there a formal grumbling strategy for them?

- Are they individuals from an expert body broadly perceived?

- Can you call an inquiry or grievance to that body?

All BSCH individuals are prepared in excellent quality. We set particular requirements for experts of hypnotherapy. Inside the online database, you will discover various sorts of participation as laid out underneath all can, in any event, a decent degree of expertise.

- Associate Member — A qualified trance specialist goes from a perceived preparing school at the Diploma/PG Cert level.

- Full Member — A qualified trance specialist goes off, in any event, Diploma/PG Cert level from a perceived school of preparing and extra authorize master preparing (for example, a Practitioner or Cognitive Behavioral level pass).

- Diplomate — As a full part, however, on an essential clinical subject with an acknowledged paper.

- Fellow — Full or Diplomatic role moved up to extraordinary administration or accomplishment from inside the general public.

To guarantee you get a confirmed and quality subliminal specialist, the different accompanying tips will manage you all the while:

Get a referral for yourself. Ask somebody you trust, similar to a companion or relative, if they have been to a trance inducer or on the off chance that they know somebody they have.

1. Ask for a referral from a qualified organization. A certified subliminal specialist might be prescribed by your PCP, chiropractor, analyst, dental specialist, or another therapeutic expert. They will likewise work with some information of your medicinal history that can enable them to prescribe a specific trance specialist in your condition.

2. Search online for a subliminal specialist. The Register of General Hypnotherapy and the American Clinical Hypnosis Society are phenomenal areas to start an inquiry. Visit roughly about six sites. A private site of trance inducers can offer you a smart thought of what they resemble, regardless of whether they explicitly spend significant time in anything and give some understanding into their systems and foundation. Check to see whether earlier patients have tributes. Ensure the site records the certifications of the trance inducers.

3. Check the protection with you. You can call them quickly and request spellbinding rehearsing specialists or another restorative workforce in your system if you have psychological wellbeing protection. You can likewise get to this information on the site of your insurance agencies. Call your state mental affiliation or state guiding affiliation and solicitation the names of confirmed clinicians or approved master advisors who rundown entrancing as one of their strengths.

4. If required, think about a long-separation arrangement. Quality over solace is consistently the best approach with regards to your wellbeing. On the off chance that you experience issues finding a gifted trance inducer in your quick district, extend your inquiry span to incorporate other neighboring urban communities or neighborhoods.

5. Ask for accreditation. No confirmed projects are gaining practical experience in hypnotherapy at noteworthy colleges. Instead, numerous trance specialists have degrees in different regions, such as drug, dentistry, or advising, and have experienced additional hypnotherapy preparation.

6. Check for training in different fields, for example, medication, brain research, or social work.

7. Be cautious about the so-called hypnotherapy specialists. They may have gotten their doctorate from an unaccredited college on the off chance that they don't have a degree in another restorative segment.

8. A believable and proficient trance specialist will have skilled office offices, inside and out entrancing information, and evidence of past clients' accomplishments.

9. Check whether the specialist is part of an association. The American Society of Clinical Hypnosis (ASCH) or the American Council of Hypnotist Examiners (ACHE) are two associations expecting members to satisfy high preparing prerequisites and have sufficient aptitudes for instruction.

10. Look at reviews for hypnotherapists on the internet. Sites, for example, Yelp, the Better Business Bureau, will have star appraisals and give patient audits that can help you show signs of improvement idea of how the advisor is and what the degree of fulfillment of her customers is.

11. Match the specialization of the therapist with your prerequisites. Hypnotherapy can be a viable pressure and tension treatment. It can likewise profit interminable agony sufferers, hot flashes, and successive migraines. Most advisors will list their strengths on their sites. However, you should also inquire as to whether they have any experience managing your particular side effects. On the off chance that you have continual back agony, for example, endeavor to discover a trance specialist who is likewise a chiropractor or general expert.

12. Ask numerous inquiries. You offer the specialist a chance to find out about you as such. You will likewise have a sentiment of how well the subliminal specialist can tune in to your prerequisites.

    • How long have they been prepared?

    • How long have they drilled?

    • The specialist should have the option of explaining the differentiation between things—for example, formal and casual stupor and what levels of consciousness they are.

13. Say the discoveries you are searching for to the specialist. A unique treatment plan ought to be imparted to you by the trance specialist, dependent on your manifestations. Be apparent about what you plan to achieve. "I need to shed pounds" or "I need to

kill ceaseless joint torment." You ought to likewise pose inquiries about your medicinal history or any past hypnotherapy experience.

14. Shop to review that you are meeting the subliminal specialist when you go to the interview to check whether they are the right fit:

    - Make sure that the trance specialist invites you.

    - Was the workplace spotless and amicable with the staff?

    - To ensure you locate the correct fit, go on a couple of discussions.

15. Finding a trance inducer trust your premonitions. At that point, feel free to arrange the event that you feel energetic or feel extraordinary about proceeding. Ensure you know and feel great with their methodology. Get some information about rates or costs and what number of visits your concern typically requires.

16. Consider pricing around. Now and then, insurance covers hypnotherapy. However, it contrasts. Check your arrangement to ensure you make an arrangement. If your insurance secures it, copayments can extend from $30 to $50 per visit. A subliminal specialist agreement could cost $50 to $275 without insurance.

Best Hypnotic Weight Loss Apps

1. Learning Self Hypnosis by Patrick Browning

This is a superb application to unwind following a long day at employment! I appreciate merely utilizing it for 30 minutes to take a portion of my day by day weight. It's exceptionally enlightening about what's mesmerizing and history. Of note is that all that you need to do in the application costs additional money.

2. Digipill

Digipill enables you to tackle your rest issue and unwind! It is also a precise instrument for getting in shape, gaining certainty, and significantly more!

3. Health and Fitness with Hypnosis, Meditation, and Music

With this basic, however fantastic application, you can get fit rapidly and keep sound. It is a helpful device that enables individuals to shed pounds by utilizing trance.

4. Harmony

Amicability is a simple method to think and unwind! You can decrease tension with this free instrument, acquire certainty, and significantly more!

5. Free Hypnosis

This free application gives you a customized mesmerizing session of your own! It is a basic, however incredible asset for simple unwinding that contains valuable strategies and activities!

6. Stress Relief Hypnosis: Anxiety, Relax and Sleep

You can unwind effectively with this spellbinding application! For those battling with sleep deprivation and nervousness, this free instrument is flawless.

Chapter 16.   Relaxation to Promote Physical Healing

Since we have seen that emotions are the first obstacle to a healthy and correct relationship with food, we are going to look specifically at the most suitable techniques to appease them. Not only that, these techniques are very important to make hypnosis deeply effective in order to achieve the desired goals.

This is all about hypnosis —in particular, the one for virtual gastric banding. In addition to hypnosis, it is worth spending a few words on autogenic training. You will thus have a technique that you can use anywhere without external aids and increase the effectiveness of hypnosis. That will lead to greater awareness of the mind-body relationship.

In fact, autogenic training is one of the techniques of self-hypnosis. What does self-hypnosis mean? As the word suggests, it is a form of self-induced hypnosis. Beyond the various methods available, all have the objective of concentrating a single thought object. To say it seems easy, but it is incredible how, in reality, our mind is constantly distracted and even overlaps distant thoughts between them. This leads to emotional tension with repercussions in everyday life.

Other self-hypnosis techniques that we will not deal with in-depth include Benson's and Erickson's.

Benson's is inspired by oriental transcendental meditation. It is based on the constant repetition of a concept in order to favor a great concentration. Specifically, he recommends repeating the word that evokes the concept several times. It is the easiest and fastest technique ever. It really takes 10-15 minutes a day. Just because it's so simple doesn't mean it's not effective, and you will also need to familiarize yourself with it, especially for those who are beginners with self-hypnosis. In fact, this could be the first technique to try right away to approach this type of practice.

You sit with your eyes closed in a quiet room and focus on breathing and relax the muscles. Therefore, continually think about the object of meditation. If your thought turns away, bring it back to the object. To be sure to practice this self-hypnosis for at least 10 minutes, just set a timer.

Erickson's is apparently more complex. The first step involves creating a new self-image that you would like to achieve. So, we start from something we don't like about ourselves and mentally create the positive image we would like to create.

In our specific case, we could start from being overweight and transforming that idea into an image of us in perfect shape, satisfied with ourselves in front of the mirror.

Then we focus on three objects around the subject, then three noises and finally three sensations. It takes little time to concentrate on these things. Gradually decrease this number. Therefore two objects, two noises and two sensations. Better if the objects are small and bright and unusual sensations, which are hardly paid attention to— for example, the feeling of the shirt that we wear in contact with our skin. You get to one, and then you leave your mind wandering. We take the negative image we have and calmly transform it mentally into the positive one. At the end of this practice, you will feel great energy and motivation.

Autogenic Training

Autogenic training is a highly effective self-induced relaxation technique without external help. It is called "training" because it includes a series of exercises that allow the gradual and passive acquisition of muscle tone changes, vascular function, cardiac and pulmonary activity, neuro-vegetative balance, and state of consciousness. But do not be frightened by this word. His exercises do not require a theoretical preparation nor a radical modification of one's habits. Practicing this activity always allows you to live a profound and repeatable experience.

Autogenic means "self-generating," unlike hypnosis and self-hypnosis, which are actively induced by an operator or the person himself.

The goal is to achieve inner harmony so that we can best face the difficulties of everyday life. It is a complementary tool for hypnosis. The two activities are intertwined. Practicing both allows a better overall experience. In fact, hypnosis helps well to act directly on the subconscious. However, for hypnosis to be effective, it is necessary to have already prepared an inner calm such that there is no resistance to the hypnotherapist's instructions. The origins of autogenic training are rooted in the activity of hypnosis. In the latter, there is an exclusive relationship between hypnotist and hypnotized. Therefore, those who are hypnotized must be in a state of maximum receptivity to reach a state of constructive passivity to create the ideal relationship with the hypnotists.

Those who approach autogenic training and have already undergone hypnosis sessions can deduce the main training guidelines from hypnosis principles. The difference is that you become your own hypnotist. Therefore, you must assume an attitude of receptive availability towards you. Such activity also allows a higher spiritual introspection, feeling masters of one's emotional state. This undoubtedly brings countless advantages in everyday life.

So, I usually suggest everyone try a hypnosis session and then do a few days of autogenic training before they start using hypnosis again daily. It is the easiest way to approach the relaxation techniques on your own and become familiar with these practices' psycho-physical sensations. Mine is a spontaneous suggestion. If you have tried meditation and relaxation techniques in the past, you can also go directly into guided hypnosis. In any case, autogenic training can be useful regardless of the level of familiarity with these practices. If you have little time in your days, it makes no sense to put so much meat on the fire. Let us remember that they are still relaxation techniques; if we see them too much as "training," we could associate obligations and bad emotions against the principle of maximum relaxation. So, I'm not saying do autogenic training and hypnosis every day, ten push-ups, crunches and maybe yoga, and then you will be relaxed and at peace with your body. This approach is not good. It is about finding your balance and harmony in a practice that must be pleasant and deliberate.

Basic Autogenic Training Exercises

The A.T.'s basic exercises are classically divided into 6 exercises, of which 2 fundamental and 4 complimentary. Before the 6 exercises, you practice an induction to calm and relaxation while ending a recovery and then awakening.

These exercises are considered as consecutive phases to be carried out in each session. It is not mandatory to carry out all the steps together. Especially initially, each exercise will have to be understood individually. But if you intend to stop, for example, in the fourth exercise and not do all of them, you will necessarily have to do the other 3 exercises in the same session first. However, the duration of the session remains unchanged because when you add exercises, you will make each phase last less. You will add the exercise when you feel you have learned the preceding one.

- **First Exercise — "The heaviness."** It's a very useful exercise to overcome psychophysical problems related to muscular tensions that derive from emotional tensions.

- **Second Exercise — "The heat."** It serves to relieve circulatory problems in all cases where there is a problem of reduced blood flow to the extremities.

- **Third Exercise — "The heart."** It is a highly suggestive exercise that allows you to regain contact with that part of the body that we traditionally deal with emotions.

- **Fourth Exercise — "The breath."** It produces better oxygenation of the blood and organs.

- **Fifth Exercise: — "The solar plexus."** It helps a lot to those who suffer from digestive problems.

- **Sixth Exercise — "The Fresh Forehead."** It produces a brain constriction vessel that can be especially useful to reduce headaches, especially if linked to physical or mental overload.

Recommended Positions

The following positions are suitable for both autogenic training and hypnosis, and relaxation techniques in general. I suggest initially to use the lying down position and to use it in hypnosis for virtual gastric bandaging to simulate the position on the surgical couch.

Lying Down

This position, at least at the beginning, is the most used for its comfort. You lie on your back (face up) and your legs slightly apart with your toes out. The arms are slightly detached from the torso and are slightly bent. The fingers are detached from each other and slightly arched.

On the Armchair

You sit with a chair attached to the wall. Your back is firmly against the backrest, and your head rests against the wall. You can place a cushion between your head and the wall.

Alternatively, you can use a high chair to rest your head-on. Legs should be flexed at 90 degrees with the feet firmly resting on them. The tips of the feet should be placed on the outside. The arms should be resting on the supports (where present) or the thighs.

If there are supports, the hands should be left dangling.

If they are not present, the hands are resting on the legs, and the fingers are separate.

Other Suggestions

To achieve the best results, the environment must be quiet, the phone and any form of technological distraction must be disconnected beforehand. There must be an incredibly soft light in the room with a constant temperature that allows neither hot nor cold. The environmental conditions, in fact, influence our mood, and the acquisition of a correct position guarantees an objective relaxation of all the muscles.

It is advisable not to wear clothes that tighten or bother you during the exercises: for this purpose, remove the watch and glasses and loosen the belt.

It goes without saying that constancy is especially important for achieving a psychic balance. It only takes 10 minutes a day, but a real reluctance is to be considered. Before doing this practice, you really need to give yourself some time. It must be deliberate practice. This is one of the reasons why it is not advisable to practice it in small time gaps between commitments but rather in dedicated time slots.

Also, it is advisable not to practice the exercises immediately after lunch to avoid sleep. At the end of each workout, perform awakening exercises except for the evening just before going to sleep.

At first, checking the relaxation of the various parts of the body will require some reflection. But over time and practice, everything will become more instinctive. Do not expect great results in the first days of practice. Do not abandon the practice immediately. Like anything else, you cannot expect to know how to do it immediately.

One last tip is not to be too picky when it comes to checking the position to take. In fact, the indications provided are broad; it is not necessary to interpret them rigidly. It must be as natural as possible, so look for what makes you feel better.

Chapter 17.   How to Lose Weight

Well, an individual can lose weight in some other effective ways. You might decide to combine them to make the processes faster and more manageable. What meditation does is that it will help you enhance some of these factors. You may find that the activities you chose to undertake become more effective as you conduct them. We do not disregard the methods; we only recommend that you complement them with meditation.

In some cases, you find that mediation can be useful on its own. While in other cases, you have to combine it with other activities to help an individual struggling with weight loss. We will go through some of the other things you might need to look at as you get on a weight loss journey. Below are some of them.

Dieting

This is perhaps the first thing we think of any time we think of weight loss. We gain weight as a result of the poor eating habits that we adopt, and they cost us a lot. Eating wrong does not only make us add weight, but it can also affect our health. We have some diseases that result from eating unhealthy foods. Plant-based meals tend to be nutritious and, at times, provide the best solution for weight loss. We shall discuss three weight-loss diets that an individual can utilize to lose weight.

Ketogenic Diet

A keto diet is a low-carb diet. It utilizes the concept of consuming high fat and the required amount of proteins while also taking a low-carb diet.

Carbohydrates are mainly composed of sugars. When we increase their consumption, we have excess sugars in the bloodstream that cannot be converted into energy. In the process, your body converts it into fats, and you end up gaining weight. A keto diet helps an individual lose weight by lowering the intake of carbohydrates. You only consume what your body requires; hence, no sugar needs to be converted into fats. You find that while using this diet, you can also burn the excess fats in your body. This works in a process known as ketosis. When the intake of glucose and other sugars is low, the body begins to convert the body's fats into energy. When this process occurs consistently, you can manage to get rid of all the excess fats, and as a result, you lose weight.

Paleo Diet

Its name was generated from the fact that it was the diet used during the Paleolithic era. If you have studied history, you probably know the events that occurred in this particular period. There were no processed foods during such times, and people would eat vegetables, fruits, seeds, nuts, and meat. There was barely any obesity case in that era since people ate what they planted or what they hunted. People came up with the ideology that if that type of diet helped people keep fit, then it can be an excellent diet to adapt to this era. Much of the weight gain is as a result of consuming food substances that are processed. They have no nutritional benefits to our bodies; instead, we drink a lot of food that has no use. We get full and satisfied after the meal, yet the body does not utilize the food. We end up gaining extra weight with no nutritional benefit. With the help of a Paleo diet, you get to consume that which you need. The body utilizes the food consumed to the maximum, and in the end, you keep fit and barely add extra weight.

Mediterranean Diet

The main inspiration behind a Mediterranean diet comes from the people living in the Mediterranean region. Some of the countries involved were Italy and Greece. Their menu was composed of fruits, unrefined cereals, vegetables, olive oil, and legumes. It also included some moderate consumption of meat, animal by-products, and wine. People using this diet were found to be healthy due to the nutrients contained in the food that they consumed. It was challenging to get diseases that result from poor eating habits. Lifestyle diseases were difficult to come by, especially this type of diet. The diet helps individuals lose weight since they get to take up what is required by the body. It also ensures that they maintain their weight. While taking this diet, you lower your carbohydrate intake. This means that you reduce your bloodstream sugar levels and that what you eat is what you require. Your body acquires the right amount of sugars, so there are no excess sugars that need to be converted into fats. That is how the Mediterranean diet helps you lose weight and have a healthy body.

How Does Meditation Help While Dieting?

You might be wondering how meditation can help while dieting and ensuring that you lose weight. Dieting can be difficult, especially if you are not disciplined enough to do so. You might find yourself having some regular cheat days, which may appear more recurrently than they should. You find that you are regularly doing this and end up not dieting at all. Meditation brings you into realizing some of the poor decisions you make as far as eating is concerned. As a result, you can make better decisions once you understand where you went wrong. Dieting can be challenging, and you need to stay focused to manage to complete the diet successfully. If you are dieting to lose weight, you need to observe the food every single day keenly. This is to help you ensure that dieting will be useful in accomplishing its purpose. In the beginning, you will face many temptations, but you can manage them with the aid of meditation. It ensures that you stay focused on the goal, and you manage to lose weight as planned.

Exercise

You might be the type of individual that immediately thinks of the gym anytime you hear about losing weight. You could believe that there is something that you physically need to do to cut off the weight. In the process, you might acquire a gym membership, and you set a gym routine whereby you get to go to the gym at certain times during the day. Even while exercising, you need meditation. Meditation allows you to concentrate on the various activities that you are undertaking. In the process, you get to give your full energy to the activities that you are taking. You find that even the various exercises that you engage in become useful in helping you lose weight. It allows you to burn the extra fats and maintains a good shape.

There is a lot of incredible power in meditation. In that calm state of mind, incredible things happen. It is more like a magical occurrence. Your account becomes keen and focused on the things that matter. In the process, you find that your performance levels are increased as you make better decisions regarding the issues at hand. This may seem like an easy thing to do, but we barely do it. An individual may find the process of meditation tedious for them to handle, yet it requires a small amount of your time. At that moment, you get to relax your mind as you think of the conditions around you. During your gym time, as you are busy exercising, you can use some of that time to meditate. This will improve your concentration and can, at times, cause you to be energized. The exercise process can get tiring, and you need to find a way to ease the burden that comes with it. With meditation, this is easily achievable.

Consuming the Necessary Amount of Food

At the time, we waste a lot of food that is not necessary. You only find that you eat because there is food to be consumed and not because you need it. With the help of meditation, there is a lot that you can accomplish. Eating when there is no need to can leads to weight gain. Your body keeps taking foods in excess quantities that it does not need. As this process progresses, you find yourself adding a lot of weight.

Meditation will help you avoid some of these incidences by helping you make the right decisions. When it comes to eating, you only do so when it is necessary.

You can plan your meals and the amount you wish to consume at a given time in a day. For instance, during breakfast, you might decide to eat a heavy meal. This is to provide you with the strength that you need to tackle the day. Breakfast is an essential meal, so you are allowed to eat slightly more than the other meals. During lunchtime, you can eat a slightly smaller portion than that of breakfast.

On the other hand, at night, you can ensure that you take the smallest part. At night there is no significant activity to be carried out unless you are working a night shift. The recommended amount you should consume should be just enough to carry you through the night. In between the day, you can include some small snacks and ensure that they are healthy snacks. If you manage to follow this keenly, your weight loss journey will be effortless. Meditation will play a significant role in ensuring that you consume the necessary amount of food and according to your meal plan.

Healthy Eating Habits

There are certain habits that we adapt to, and that contribute to weight gain. For instance, you might have a habit of eating too fast, and as a result, food is not well processed. This causes the food to become waste, and instead of benefiting your body, it becomes a problem for your organization. In some situations, you might find that what you consumed had some nutritious benefits, but due to your poor eating habits, it does not help you in the way that it should. At times, you might cook a lot of food or even serve yourself a lot of food. You might get to a point whereby you feel like you are already full. However, you keep eating because there is food on your plate or because you have some leftover food. The excess food you consume once you are full will not help your body, so you can find yourself adding weight.

Chapter 18.   Blasting Calories

We have all heard the word "calorie" and its relation to our body weight—calories contained in the foods we consume and often misunderstood about how they affect us. We seek to explain what they are, how to count them, and the best methods of blasting them to avoid weight gain.

What Are Calories, and How Do They Affect Your Weight?

A calorie is a fundamental estimating unit. For example, we use meters when communicating separation; 'Usain Bolt went 100 meters in merely 9.5 seconds.' There are two units in this expression. One is a meter (a range unit), and the other is "second" (a period unit). Necessarily, calories are additional units of substantial amount estimation.

Many assume that a calorie is the weight measure (since it is frequently connected with an individual's weight). However, that is not precise; a calorie is a vitality unit (estimation). One calorie is proportional to the vitality expected to build the temperature by 1 °C to 1 kilogram of water.

Two particular sorts of calories come in: small calories and massive calories. Huge calories are the word connected to sustenance items.

You've likely observed much stuff on parcels (chocolates, potato chips, and so forth) with 'calorie scores.' Imagine the calorie score an incentive for a thing being '100 cal.' This infers when you eat it, you will pick up about as much vitality (even though the calorie worth expressed and the amount you advantage from it is never the equivalent).

All we eat has a particular calorie tally; it is the proportion of the vitality we eat in the substance bonds.

These are mostly things we eat: starches, proteins, and fats. How about we take a gander at what number of calories 1 gram comprises of these medications: 1 Sugar 4 calories 2. Protein–3 calories. Fat–9 calories.

Are My Calories Awful?

That is fundamentally equivalent to mentioning, "Is vitality awful for me?" Every single activity the body completes needs vitality. Everything takes energy to stand, walk, run, sit, and even eat. In case you're doing any of these tasks, it suggests you're utilizing vitality, which mostly infers you're 'consuming' calories, explicitly the calories that entered your body when you were eating some nourishment.

To sum things up, for you, NO... calories are not terrible.

Equalization is the way to find harmony between the number of calories you devour and what number of calories you consume. On the off chance that you eat fewer calories and spend more, you will become dainty. In contrast, on the opposite side, on the off chance that you gobble up heaps of calories, however, you are a habitually lazy person. You will, in the long run, become stout at last.

Each movement we do throughout a day will bring about sure calories spent. Here is a little rundown of the absolute most much of the time performed exercises, just as the number of calories consumed while doing them.

Step-By-Step Instructions to Count Calories

You have to expend fewer calories than you consume to get thinner.

This clamor is simple in principle. Be that as it may, it very well may be hard to deal with your nourishment admission in the contemporary sustenance setting. Calorie checking is one approach to address this issue and is much of the time used to get more fit. Hearing that calories don't make a difference is very common, and tallying calories is an exercise in futility. Nonetheless, calories tally with regards to weight; this is a reality in which, in science, analyses called overloading studies have demonstrated numerous occasions.

These examinations request that people deliberately indulge and, after that, survey the impact on their weight and wellbeing. All overloading investigations have found that people are putting on weight when they devour a more significant number of calories than they consume.

This simple reality infers that calorie checking and limiting your utilization can be proficient in averting weight put on or weight reduction as long as you can stick to it. One examination found that health improvement plans, including calorie, including brought about an average weight reduction of around 7 lbs. (3.3 kg) more than those that didn't.

Primary concern: you put on weight by eating a more significant number of calories than you consume. Calorie tallying can help you expend fewer calories and get more fit.

How Many Calories Do You Have to Eat?

The number of calories that you need depends on factors such as sex, age, weight, and measure of activity. In case you're endeavoring to get in shape, by eating not correctly your body consumes off, you'll have to construct a calorie deficiency. Utilize this adding machine to decide what number of calories you ought to expend every day (opening in crisp tab). This number cruncher depends on the condition of Mifflin-St Jeor, an exact method to evaluate calorie prerequisites.

How to Reduce Your Caloric Intake for Weight Loss

Bit sizes have risen, and a solitary dinner may give twofold or triple what the regular individual needs in a sitting at certain cafés. "Segment mutilation" is the term used to depict huge parts of sustenance as the standard. It might bring about weight put on and weight reduction. In general, people don't evaluate the amount they spend. Tallying calories can help you battle indulging by giving you more grounded information about the amount you expend.

In any case, you have to record portions of sustenance appropriately for it to work. Here are a couple of well-known strategies for estimating segment sizes:

- **Scales.** Weighing your sustenance is the most exact approach to decide the amount you eat. This might be tedious, in any case, and isn't always down to earth.

- **Estimating Cups.** Standard estimations of amount are, to some degree, quicker and less complex to use than a scale, yet can some of the time be tedious and unbalanced.

- **Examinations.** It's quick and easy to utilize correlations with popular items, especially if you're away from home. However, it's considerably less exact.

Contrasted with family unit items, here are some mainstream serving sizes that can gauge your serving sizes:

- 1 serving of rice or pasta (1/2 a cup): a PC mouse or adjusted bunch.

- 1 Meat serving (3 oz): a card deck.

- 1 Fish serving (3 oz): visit book.

- 1 Cheese serving (1.5 oz): a lipstick or thumb size.

- 1 Fresh organic product serving (1/2 cup): a tennis ball.

- 1 Green verdant vegetable serving (1 cup): baseball ball.

- 1 Vegetable serving (1/2 cup): a mouse PC.

- 1 Olive oil teaspoon: 1 fingertip.

- 2 Peanut margarine tablespoons: a ping pong ball.

Calorie tallying, notwithstanding when gauging and estimating partitions, isn't an exact science.

In any case, your estimations shouldn't be thoroughly spot-on. Simply guarantee that your utilization is recorded as effectively as would be prudent. You should be mindful of marking high-fat as well as sugar things, for example, pizza, dessert, and oils. Under-recording these meals can make an enormous qualification between your genuine and recorded utilization. You can endeavor to utilize scales toward the beginning to give you an excellent idea of what a segment resembles to upgrade your evaluations. This should help you to be increasingly exact, even after you quit utilizing them.

More Tips to Assist in Caloric Control

Here are five more calorie tallying tips:

- Get prepared: get a calorie counting application or web device before you start, choose how to evaluate or gauge parcels, and make a feast plan.

- Read nourishment marks: food names contain numerous accommodating calorie tallying information. Check the recommended segment size on the bundle.

- Remove the allurement: dispose of your home's low-quality nourishment. This will help you select more advantageous bites and make hitting your objectives easier.

- Aim for moderate, steady loss of weight: don't cut too little calories. Even though you will get in shape all the more rapidly, you may feel terrible and be less inclined to adhere to your arrangement.

- Fuel your activity: diet and exercise are the best health improvement plans. Ensure you devour enough to rehearse your vitality.

Effective Methods for Blasting Calories

To impact calories requires participating in exercises that urge the body to utilize vitality. Aside from checking the calories and guaranteeing you eat the required sum, consuming them is similarly essential for weight reduction. Here, we examine a couple of techniques that can enable you to impact our calories all the more viably:

1. Indoor cycling: McCall states that around 952 calories for each hour should be 200 watts or higher. On the off chance that the stationary bicycle doesn't demonstrate watts: "*this infers you're doing it when your indoor cycling instructor educates you to switch the opposition up!*" he proposes.

2. Skiing: around 850 calories for every hour depends on your skiing knowledge. Slow, light exertion won't consume nearly the same number of calories as a lively, fiery effort wasted. To challenge yourself and to consume vitality? Attempt to ski tough.

3. Rowing: approximately 816 calories for every hour. The benchmark here is 200 watts; McCall claims it ought to be at a "fiery endeavor." many paddling machines list the showcase watts. Reward: rowing is additionally a stunning back exercise.

4. Jumping rope: *about 802 calories for each hour this ought to be at a moderate pace*—around 100 skips for each moment—says McCall. Attempt to begin with this bounce rope interim exercise.

5. Kickboxing: approximately 700 calories for every hour. Also, in this class are different sorts of hand-to-hand fighting, for example, Muay Thai with regards to standard boxing, when you are genuine in the ring (a.k.a. Battling another individual), the

most significant calorie consumption develops. Be that as it may, many boxing courses add cardio activities, for example, hikers and burpees, so your pulse will, in the long run, increase more than you would anticipate. What's more, hello, before you can get into the ring, you need to start someplace, isn't that so?

6. Swimming: approximately 680 calories per hour freestyle works. However, as McCall says, *you should go for a vivacious 75 yards for each moment.* For an easygoing swimmer, this is somewhat forceful. (Butterfly stroke is significantly progressively productive if you extravagant it.)

7. Outdoor bicycling: approximately 680 calories for each hour biking at a fast, lively pace will raise your pulse, regardless of whether you are outside or inside. Add to some rocky landscape and mountains, and it gets significantly more calorie-consuming.

The volume of calories devoured is straightforwardly proportionate to the measure of sustenance, just like the kind of nourishment an individual expends. The best way to reduce calories is by being cautious about what you devour and captivating in dynamic physical exercises to consume an overabundance of calories in your body.

Chapter 19. Weight Control Individualization

Individualization of a particular program is being stressed, and more of this is still going to happen. If you want the plan you choose to work with to be most effective and produce beautiful results, you must make it yours and ensure that it is unique to you according to what you think can work well for you. Do not start using a not individualized program, one that you pick from anywhere, and start using because it may not work for you. As you already know, as an individual, you have a unique retinal pattern, fingerprints, and the body chemistry you have does not match anyone else. The things you have experienced in life are also different from those of other people.

In the same way, a program that you can use to help you in attaining a unique bodyweight should also be unique to you so that it can achieve maximum positive results. This is why you can see that here you are only provided with a few meditation exercises that you have the chance to choose the best ones that suits you. Giving you so many meditation exercises may be overwhelming when choosing the activity that suits your body and the one you are comfortable with. When you are overwhelmed with many choices of meditation exercises to choose from, there is the possibility that you may be confused about making the right decision. Also, you can see that no meditation has been given in a stone manner; the only part that you need to put a lot of effort to ensure success is maintaining your discipline and telling yourself that you know the kind of goals you want. It would be best if you achieved them no matter what happens as you proceed with these exercises.

As an individual, you should discover which form suits you best and follow that diligently until you get the results you aim for. Many people all over the world have tried meditation methods. Still, many of them have failed because most meditational schools believe that there is one way to meditate, which applies to each and everyone throughout the world. Many think that they have learned this method from their meditation schools and their teacher through coincidence and by being curious. But the truth is that this could be their best meditation method as individuals, but it does not mean everyone else will find it comfortable, and by using it, they must achieve success. Such people who have been disappointed because they did not get the results they expected from the meditation exercises believe that it cannot work for them, yet they have not tried other forms of meditation and see how it can work for them.

However, particular aspects come in all forms of meditational paths. For example, meditators should try to continually arrive at the maximum attention possible, which is called coherent attention in some meditational schools. This is whereby, as an individual, you decide to discipline your mind and ensure always to do one thing at a particular time to maintain focus and avoid being overwhelmed. You also decide that you love yourself, and you will treat yourself in a manner that you have promised yourself. These are some of the constants when it comes to various meditational schools. Apart from these, the other things involved like doing your meditation while walking in the area of your comfort, doing it while sitting in an armchair, and lying on the floor are things that you should decide for yourself and consider the one that you are comfortable with. When it comes to deciding the best time for you to perform the meditational exercises, it is up to you, and there is no conventional way in which you should follow. You can choose to be doing it either once or twice a day and perform them for one, two, or three weeks depending on what you have promised yourself that you will achieve.

As you continue, if you find that you are committed and have a great desire to achieve the healthy bodyweight you need to have, you can decide to follow all the meditational exercises because overall, they will help you achieve your goals. If you do not want to try different meditational paths, you can decide to go for the combined meditations you have explicitly identified. There are various forms of meditation that you can choose to go with. Some of these meditational paths include those that stress on the intellectual path, that those enable you to work through emotions, and others that religious groups in the western world have devised. It does not matter the form of meditation you have decided to use to attain your goals and experience fulfillment. The truth is that to achieve what you want with these various kinds of meditations. You must put in the work that is required. The results will not be easy for any form of meditation that you decide to go with. Be sure that whatever path you choose, you will not find any easy path because achieving the growth and development you want is difficult. The only best way to achieve what you want is to be serious and be prepared to put in an effort that will not stop soon.

These statements may seem to be put strongly, but those who have attempted to change their lives and succeeded can attest to this and tell you that it is the truth. When we work to achieve a healthy body weight through meditation, we need to know that we will individualize our meditational programs and other aspects of our lives that we should also individualize. We will look at some of these things that we should put into consideration when it comes to individualizing the program we have.

For many years, individualization has not been taken seriously, and many have underrated it. Even some experienced psychiatrists do not seem to get it, and many of them may not understand that various patients need different help when it comes to psychotherapy. These people also need various preparedness measures to deal with impending stress due to surgery, and they should be helped differently so that they can effectively deal with allergies, grief, and other issues affecting their lives. But the modern concept does not need to incorporate this hence the reason you see why many meditations have been conditioned to think that there is a particular method of performing psychotherapy that is correct and can be used on various patients, and this is the method that they learned from their teachers and mastered it carefully.

Those who try to come up with different concepts, both meditation teachers and patients, do not succeed in convincing others that there is a need for an individualized program for everyone to work well and for the patient to succeed. Many find it easy to believe that there is only one way regardless of what you are dealing with, whether it is meditation, psychotherapy, or other things that need treatment.

They do not want to face the complex situation that every one of different, and the best way is to deal with each individual differently, whether this is something complicated or not. However, it would help if you got that we are different individuals with different bodies. When thinking of exercises, do not go for what has been hyped but design your individualized program because this can help you get the best results and follow your journey to becoming what you want to become. Are you thinking of changing the movement exercise that you have been doing? If you do not have such an exercise you are doing currently, you can add it to your daily program. By looking around, try to know what is appealing to you. You can find an exercise that you are happy with. The kind of exercise you choose should be one that you are left feeling good after you are through with the performance. If you are good with the popular exercise at the moment, you can go for it, and this could be a sweet coincidence. As you choose the exercise, you need to consider some factors like your current age, the pattern of exercises you were engaged in, and your physique. If you are okay with it, you may decide to combine several of these exercises and add them to the specific regimen you already have. You may choose to be jogging every morning, swimming a few laps on two days of the week, and taking a walk on days like Sundays.

As you may have already realized, the subject of the right path for each person, lacking, has been stressed. Meditation is also not left out, which is one of the best ways to solve various individuals' issues. It is excellent for many great people worldwide who have appreciated many people but remember that some people find it relevant and not that helpful in their lives. If you are devoted to these meditational exercises and conscientiously perform them for a period of six to eight weeks without seeing results, do not hate yourself because meditation is not your thing. By doing it, your weight cannot become worse, but even if you do not notice the benefits that you were looking for, the advantage that will be there is that you will have undertaken something that you have not done before. At the same time, you will also have engaged your mind to know various things that maybe you did not know about yourself and your body. Even when you find that meditation may not work best when it comes to solving your weight problem, the experience is beneficial, and it will help you learn a lot.

Chapter 20.   Quick Way to Burn Fat

Have you ever found the safest and easiest way to efficiently burn fat and lose weight without working off your butt and getting starving to death? I have, and that's precisely why I've been looking for a long time for the safest and easiest way to burn fat quickly! Here's what I got.

A lot of people are struggling to lose weight, and there are many reasons for this:

Some have a prolonged metabolism, and the fats in the foods they eat every day do not break down properly and store as body fat, which causes an excess of fat and constant weight gains.

Some people lead an unhealthy lifestyle because it has something to do with their job at the moment. It may not involve much physical activity, or because they want to sit and snack on various types of foods that slow down the metabolism, and they get used to that kind of lifestyle before they know it.

An important explanation for why some people gain weight is because of excessive sugar consumption or simply because the amount of sugar in their blood is naturally high and allows them to gain weight. Certain high levels and types of sugar cause diabetes, which is a major factor and a significant issue behind unnecessary weight gain. There are many weight loss plans out there that tell you different simple ways to lose fat rapidly, and most of them don't work because they don't make things easier for any particular situation like diabetes, eating patterns, and so on. Drink Hot Tea. Although it's not clear how this occurs, researchers seem to have found that drinking 6 cups of cold water a day will increase the metabolism of bodies by about 50 calories a day. This is roughly the equivalent of 5 pounds a year being shredded. Now that does not sound like a lot, but it's a smart thing to lose those extra pounds, given that it's all done by drinking water only. Perhaps the safest way is to drink filtered or distilled water rather than tap water.

Eat a Little Sun

It has been found that the chemical capsicum present in chili peppers lights up the metabolism. A Food Science and Vitamin Logy Journal report suggests adding chili peppers improves your metabolism and lets you consume more calories. Keep any handy to add to a plate, or use red-pepper flakes to spice up a favorite sauce.

Breakfast Is Served Every Morning

Fact, breakfast is the main meal of the day. Eating a healthy breakfast ensures that after a long night's sleep, the metabolism goes. People who miss breakfast are almost fivefold more likely to become obese. When a good meal doesn't activate the morning's metabolism, the body has no real choice but to hold onto fat reserves.

Will That Be Tea or Coffee?

Yeah, caffeine is known to help improve metabolism. A cup of brewed tea has been demonstrated to enhance metabolism by 12%. Researchers assume that this boost is provided by the antioxidant called Catechins in the drink. Only note, when making your coffee, avoid artificial sweeteners or sugar and take it straight up. Evite the lattes in your nearest coffee shop too. They can taste sweet, but some may contain as much as 700 calories. That's about 1/3 of your average total caloric intake for the day.

Eat and Battle Fat Food

It has shown that people who eat at least 25 grams of fiber a day burn fat by as much as 30%. This is almost equivalent to three daily servings of fruits and vegetables. You can also get whole-grain fiber from you. Just be aware that all these grains come from sprouted grains, such as millet, spelled, and quinoa. Stop highly processed whole wheat loaves of bread, entire wheat kinds of pasta, and the like, which are considered "clean." When you eat these, all they do is turn to sugar in the digestive tract, resulting in exceptional fat content.

In the fight against weight gain, the mind is a potent weapon. The trick is getting into an attitude that is going to drive you when things get tough. If you're able to persuade yourself that your target is achievable, you'll win half the battle. Most people give up on this because it is too difficult. If things get rough, or you want to throw them in the towel, take a step back and slow things down. Often the stuff of time is all in mind, and you'll see results if you can monitor your thoughts on this matter.

The Start Stage

Any journey, no matter how long and how complicated, begins with step number one. This may sound like a cliché, but it is genuinely absolute. You can go miles and miles down a path, and you'll finally get to your destination if you keep driving. Painting this image is only one thing you can keep in mind when you step on to try to change things for good.

Take an evaluation of your eating habits and your workout schedule to begin with. If you don't have any, then the first step is to analyze what you do. Write down what you always eat and what your favorite food is. For others, that will seem complicated or even arduous, but it will benefit you in the long run. If you don't see what it is, you can't solve a problem.

Improving Your Lifestyle

The only way to lose weight is by the change in lifestyle. It is not through diets that you induce pain, it is not through hunger, and for most people, it is not by surgical means. It starts with changing your way of looking at the food. It would help if you learned how to balance things a little better, instead of indulging whenever you like. The balancing act you can build for your life can force you to reconsider what food is and how to burn pure fat.

Some naturally occurring foods can increase the metabolism rate and cause you to lose fat cells when you don't even do anything. Imagine making the cells in your body chugging around, resting, and eating pure fat cells. This can improve by proper nutrition, and it starts with the lifestyle decisions swapped out.

This could be as easy as consuming more fruits, consuming fewer at dinner time, and enjoying new recipes with whole foods, grains, nuts, and berries. Scaling back on sugar drinks, like energy drinks, may help achieve this lifestyle change target. It need not be a 180-degree turn, and it can be incremental.

Instead of telling you just to hit the gym and get more exercise, the goal here is to try. Seek to find a minimum of 30 minutes of your schedule to devote to some activity during the day. You may not need to prepare for a triathlon in the first few weeks or something like that. With just a 30 minute walk out of your day, you can launch your project. You can start by walking the road or finding a local track. Try jogging slowly as you get better and better at this, and finally start running.

Find another fitness plan for those who don't like the technique that you need, whether it's a DVD set or joining a class to learn kung fu; fitness matters. If you combine the power of fitness with the power of exercise, you can see yourself in a whole new light and lose weight even more quickly. You could also learn something about yourself in the process and what you love about exercising. It can be not easy at first to find something that you want, but if you stick to it, you'll find your life-changing for the better.

Health traps exercise is one thing to avoid. If you cannot lift 500 pounds, for example, or cannot run 10 miles physically, don't. Do not drive yourself to positions where you'll be hurt—stepping up the exercise levels slowly and taking time to be healthy. Health matters a lot, so don't think you have to risk yourself to lose weight and burn fat, because that isn't real.

Ways in Which Constructive Thinking Reconfigures the Subconscious Mind

Whether or not we know, our minds are divided into two parts—the conscious and the subconscious. The conscious mind governs our everyday activities and receives a surge of feelings and sensations that determine our daily attitudes and acts. In contrast, the subconscious mind is the protector of our deep, pre-existing set of beliefs that have been at the deepest level of our brains since early childhood. These unconscious, deep-seated beliefs play an enormous role in sending thoughts to the conscious mind, and more importantly, feelings.

Unfortunately, most of us were unconsciously hardwired to transmit negative, restricting thoughts and feelings from the subconscious mind to the conscious mind resulting in less than favorable results about happiness, relationships, health, and wealth. The happiest, most successful people in the world are those who have learned how to master and rewire to their advantage their subconscious minds, thus manifesting lives of joy, perfect health, abundance, and success.

Chapter 21.   How the Mind Works

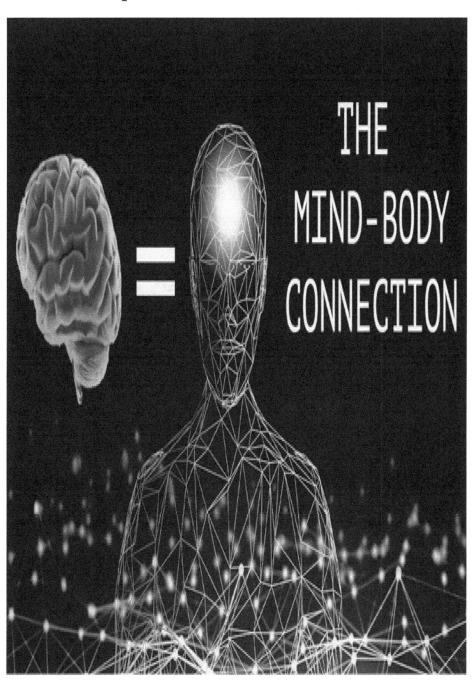

It is imperative and essential to know what kind of thought you fix and digest into your mind because these are what form the basis of your belief system and your type of experiences. Thoughts can either be positive or negative but in all, nurture your mind with the right and positive kind of ideas, happiness, goodness, love, peace, giving, big-heartedness, humility, and lots more.

A friend of mine has been in a mess for about fifteen years now, which causes her pain due to the fact she thinks she's not good enough to look upon. She was lost and in the aura of this low esteem belief for quite fifteen years that seem quite long, right? At her tender age, her mother seems to be going through some tough times and moments in the family, which was highly traumatic; hence, cultivating habits like overeating, drinking, and smoking. These habits got her ballooned in stature. The mother didn't want to reveal to her daughter (my friend) that she was passing through hard times emotionally; instead, she engaged in smoking, overeating, and drinking as a measure of escape from others knowing her exact problem.

My friend has got to emulate, is her mother, and having lived together for long, she imbibed and taught her mother's habits, not coming to the consciousness of the adverse effects. These habits didn't mean anything special to my friend because that was her upbringing. It has become a norm to her, therefore not seeing anything to caution about her diet. It wasn't the joy of the mother to feed herself to stupor, but that's all got to override her emotional trauma, which has also been regulated and fixed in her subconscious mind, even when she's not intentional about taking a bulk of food, she sees herself in it unknowingly.

After discovering that a transformation was necessary for her life, mental faculty and belief system were the vital things to be addressed because

144

these formed the contents of her subconscious mind. In turn, it has been a persuasive deprivation from her losing weight.

If I may ask you a question; do you want to lose weight? There is this quick prompting to answer 'YES,' this answer that possibly may come from your conscious mind, but what is your subconscious mind saying? Is it also saying 'YES'? Because if any change must happen at all, there is a need for a synergy between the conscious and the subconscious mind. The collaborative effort of the two targeted or focused in the same direction affects the change, knowing the essence of the soul's pleasing effect towards achieving a weight loss. Therefore, it is necessary to understand how to put the mid together in a direction for a specific purpose.

There are several journals, articles, and materials on the science of the mind and behavior, which is the mental or behavioral characteristics of an individual; also, check out books on spiritual practices, growth, guidance, and counseling as a self-help measure. Although, just a few out of most the books on mind talk and clearly explain how the brain works concerning personal growth. It may take a decision sometimes to change things.

In the regulation of the brain, advice from psychologists is pretty cool and useful. We should put our minds together in the right order. Thoughts form the baseline of constructive and destructive behaviors. Learning the systematic nature of our beliefs is equivalent to finding the secrets of human psychology. Our exposure to the radiance of the right knowledge and understanding alongside the wisdom of mind functionality is the straight route to our liberation. At first, the basis of it all is a concrete understanding of how the human mind and consciousness work in totality.

It understands the operation of the subconscious mind.

Consciousness literally refers to one's notice of one's particular thoughts, memories, feelings, environments and sensations. Knowledge is one's awareness of one's self and the environment around you. The notice you have is relative and unique to you. When a person is said to have the ability to describe what he's going through in words verbally, then he is conscious. Change is constant when it comes to conscious experience. For instance, presently, you may be focused on reading a billboard post, and another time one's consciousness may shift to the discussion you had some time ago with the boss, and after that, the speed of your fan may catch your attention. Your knowledge of the continuous change of focus from one time to the other is consciousness.

The two essential states of awareness are conscious and subconscious. They are the two main divisions that constitute the human mind based on the local divisions. The conscious mind deals with everything that pertains to awareness. It is the part of our mental processing that makes us a reason and with understanding.

The conscious functions include critical and analytical thinking, logical reasoning, decisive ability, sensations, feelings, perceptions, and short-live memory. The subconscious entails the things we hardly think about in the present but can dive into the conscious mind. It addresses our biological systems and how we maintain responses coupled with long-term memory.

The conscious mind contains just 10% and the subconscious 90% of the fraction of the brain. Hence, it should be known that the surest way to change life is to learn to control your mind at the level of the subconscious.

Subconscious Mind Expositions

The subconscious mind often obeys our directives. How do I mean? This implies whatever command you give to it is what you receive in return. There will be a lot of trouble if it not programmed in our favor, and we can gain the benefits if we get the correct commands. It will, of course, receive inputs and discover what is stimulated by our emotions. The subconscious mind is a useful messenger but a terrible master. Everything either needed or not is achieved once we have confirmed the related emotions. The higher the intensity of the feelings we receive, the more efficient and promptly we can get goals delivered. How is it processed? The thought forms an image; an image forms emotion, and the feeling, therefore, births a reality. Consequently, it could mean that we create our ideas based on whatever we've seen, received or once inputted into our mind. However, this connotes that we determine or control what comes into our subconscious mind.

Many things have formed the basis of our dispositions due to what has imbibed in us from a very tender age. What we listen to, what we say and what we think is always a resultant effect of the ideas we have taught from our childhood stage. The views are what form the reasons behind every decision we take; instead of focusing on solutions and way out, we tend to attack what is not necessary.

When a child steals, some parents, especially in some part of the world, believe flogging the thief out of the child is the only solution. Even when they have given profitable alternatives and measures to help the child, they still resolve severe and severe beating. The big question is: are they interested in the defeat of the child or the change? It's so unfortunate that the first decision of punishment comes to our mind rather than the change we indeed want to see. The penalty is now the focus, not the difference. As we declare or think of a word, it forms an image in our head, thereby generating stronger emotions in us.

Take, for instance, if I tell you not to imagine a blue orange. What just happened? You picture it right. However, it is very important to know that words can go a long way if they're registered in your mind, whether negative or positive, because the mind does not understand negations. Also, if you want to input something into your brain, be focused on imagining the related scene, either in the past or present because it gives you an image of the future.

Your conscious mind is always engaged because your brain is busy incorporating words seen on the text's pages on your eyeballs and interpreting them into useful information, but your inner consciousness is undoubtedly at work. It's processing what you have read and stored a portion of it as a piece of information that will serve as a reference in the future through memory. The gathering of this processed information results in how we understand and relate to things in the future.

Work has been tediously put to place by neuroscientists and psychologists to get the subconscious mind's rigid and tangible features.

It is generally known that the brain consists of a series of a network called synapses. The moment we have the thought of anything, the charge flows from one neuron to the others along with this network. Hence, we can change our brain—that is learning and incorporating things or fresh memories by changing this network.

The reason why we will wash dishes, and suddenly an idea pops up through our mind is because even when we aren't taking note of this network with consciousness, they are yet in our brains.

The field of science isn't too particular on how and why this occurs; for sure, I know the entrepreneurs can affirm the power embedded in subconscious ideas. Of course, few strategies can be put in place to enhance the quality functioning of the brain.

We possibly can't determine what happens to us; we can only determine or control how we respond to it. It can be argued that the ability or inability of the entrepreneurs to react correctly to the market will be the sole factor of their success. There is no doubt that we struggle with our reactions, which come to play as emotions, fears, aspirations, and goals. These can influence how we respond to situations.

Chapter 22. Why You Should Stop Emotional Eating?

We don't know we're an emotional eater for most of us, or we don't think it's that severe. For some of us, it doesn't lead to feelings of shame or weight gain. We can console some of us and think it's not a big deal, but it's not.

Among others, emotional eating is out of balance, something that can dominate our everyday lives. This may seem like overwhelming cravings or hunger, but it's just the feeling that we feel hungry, helpless, and add to our weight.

Comfort food gives us immediate pleasure and takes away feeling. Digestion and sensation require a lot of time, and the body can't do it. Comfort eating helps us to suppress pain because we flood our digestive tract with poisonous waste.

When we feel anxious, feeling a big empty hole inside us like we're hungry can be natural. Instead of confronting what this means— i.e. our emotions—we're stuffing it down. In culture, it seems we are afraid to feel too much that we don't even know we're running from our feelings much of the time.

If we don't let ourselves react, we'll repress it. You will feel exhausted until you begin to let yourself feel the thoughts or feelings that emerge and avoid stuffing down. It is because the body releases past pent-up emotions, and it can strike you hard.

That's why it can be hard to let go of emotional eating, as we have to conquer the initial "scare" to move on and start learning to accept emotions for what they are. To be present, allowing a feeling to wash over us is wonderful and should be appreciated.

The more you allow yourself to be in the present moment and feel, the fewer feelings that overtake you, the less terrified you will be. The emotion's strength also decreases. You'll become mentally and physically stronger. When it's off your stomach, you'll feel so much better than replacing it with food.

Getting to this point isn't fast. Some people can split their emotional eating by better nourishing their body to get rid of physical cravings and supporting others when they feel anxious or emotional.

To stop emotional eating, you must be mindful of how and why you eat—taking a day out to consider what makes you happy. Many people don't even understand real hunger!

When you're eating, mentally, can you stop yourself?

Could you sit and let the emotion wash over you instead of eating-give yourself time to feel it and transfer it? Or would you talk to someone about how you feel?

Don't injure yourself.

Emotional eating is usually something you've done from an early age because it's part of your make-up. It's a practiced habit, so you've learned to cope with the environment.

It takes time to undo something so ingrained in you, so if you find yourself eating out of guilt—if you mess up—learn from it, just move on.

Recognition is the first step. If you know you eat safely, you can conquer it.

Journaling will also help you recognize eating habits. Note down before, during, and after a meal. What caused eating? Was real hunger?

To learn how to avoid emotional eating, I can help. For years, I suffered from an emotional eating epidemic, sometimes going on a day-to-day binge eating marathon. I never really understood what caused these eating outbursts; all I knew was that I would start eating and not stop until the food was gone or anyone near me saw me.

The situation escalated, and my weight started to increase. Any diet I was on would instantly fail, and my self-confidence reached an all-time low. My eating causes were thought to be related to work stress, but so many others may play a part. Relationships, depression, financial difficulties, and many others will easily consume binge sequences.

When I started trying to figure out how to avoid emotional eating, I didn't know where to start. Like you, I went online and started investigating. I spent the whole day reading, digesting, and gathering emotional cure knowledge, then around 3 a.m. I found my savior that morning.

How Can You Avoid Emotional Eating?

The answer is very easy. The trick is identifying the real root cause of the problems and addressing those root causes. You may think it is tension or job issues. Yet mental eating disorders are also much more profound than on the surface. Following the root, a cause can quickly treat these symptoms and safely cure your binge eating.

Mental eating satisfies your mental appetite. It's not about your kitchen, but the issue lies in your head. What are the most powerful emotional eating challenge strategies?

List Your Food Cravings to Relax

Distracting yourself doesn't mean being lazy in this situation. It's not like texting while driving, or you're out of control. When you hide from your food cravings, it means you're turning your focus to something else. It's more purposeful.

Do something or concentrate on another action or event. Whenever you feel like gorging food, try getting a piece of paper and list five items from five categories of something like the names of five people whenever you feel upset, angry, or depressed.

Perhaps you should mention five ways to relax. If you want to calm down, what are your five places?

When anxious, what five feel-good phrases can you tell yourself? How about five things to stop eating?

Place on your fridge or kitchen cabinet after finishing this list. Next time you're overwhelmed by your persuasive food cravings, browse through your list and do one of the 25 things suggested there.

Prepare Ahead for Future Emotional Issues

Over the weekend, grab a piece of paper and a pencil and take a path to your tasks in the days ahead. Your map reveals your expected exits and potential detours. Pick an emotionally consuming picture.

Place the icon over an event or activity that could cause your food cravings, like early lunch with your in-laws. Prepare ahead for that case. Search for the restaurant menu online to order something delicious and nutritious.

Drop the Concerns Inside

Whenever anxious, taking a deep breath helps. Another thing to detoxify yourself from stress is to do a visual trick. Breathe deeply and imagine a squeegee (that scraping implement you use to clean your window or windshield) near your eyes. Slowly breathe out, picture the squeegee wiping clean inside. Delete all your concerns. Do it three times.

Self-talk like you're royalty. Self-criticism is usually emotional. Toxic words you say to yourself, such as "I'm such a loser" or "I can never seem to do anything right," force you to drive to the nearest. Don't be fooled by these claims though brief.

Such feelings, like acid rain, slowly erode your well-being. The next time you're caught telling yourself these negative things, overcome by moving to a third-person perspective.

If you think "I'm such a mess," tell yourself then that "Janice is such a mess, but Janice will do what it takes to get things done and make herself happy."

This approach will get you out of the negative self-talk loop and have some perspective. Pull up, be positive, have the strength, and avoid emotional eating.

Over-food is still not given enough consideration. It's always seen as not a serious problem to laugh at.

This is an incorrect view as a horrific condition needing urgent treatment. The positive thing is that you take action to help you avoid emotional eating forever. I know because I did it myself.

Step 1 — Recognize triggers

For each person, emotional eating is triggered differently. Some people get cravings when stressed out, some when depressed or bored. You need to try and work out the emotional causes. When you know what they are, you'll get early notice when the urge to feed comes on you.

Step 2 — Eliminate Temptation

One thing most people don't realize about emotional eating is that desire is always for one specific food. It's always ice-cream or candy for kids. It's still pizza for guys.

When you couldn't fulfill this lure, it won't bother you. Save your home from all of these temptations.

Throw out any nearby pizza delivery locations. Again, you know your tempters, so get rid of them and make overeating difficult.

Step 3 — Break Contact

It's instant and urgent when craving hits. You're fed RIGHT NOW! To stop this, you must break this immediate bond by taking some time between desires and eating.

Call a friend Count to 60

Write down what you feel like

Do some exercises, go out for a walk

Take a shower

What you can do to make the urge subside do wonder.

Take these three moves, and you'll soon take them better and conquer emotional eating for good.

Chapter 23.   Hypnosis Myths

It is common to misjudge the topic of hypnotism. That is why myths and half-truths abound about this matter.

Myth 1. You Won't Recall Anything That Happened When You Were Mesmerized When You Wake up From a Trance

While amnesia may occur in uncommon cases, people more often than not recollect everything that unfolded during mesmerizing. Mesmerizing, be that as it may, can have a significant memory impact. Posthypnotic amnesia may make an individual overlook a portion of the stuff that occurred previously or during spellbinding. This effect, be that as it may, is typically confined and impermanent.

Myth 2. Hypnosis Can Help People to Recall the Exact Date of Wrongdoing They Have Been Seeing

While spellbinding can be utilized to improve memory, the effects in well-known media have been significantly misrepresented. Research has discovered that trance doesn't bring about noteworthy memory improvement or precision, and entrancing may, in reality, lead to false or misshaped recollections.

Myth 3. You Can Be Spellbound Against Your Will

Spellbinding needs willful patient investment regardless of stories about people being mesmerized without their authorization.

Myth 4. While You Are Under a Trance, the Trance Specialist Has Full Power over Your Conduct

While individuals frequently feel that their activities under trance appear to happen without their will's impact, a trance specialist can't make you act against your wants.

Myth 5. You Might Be Super-Solid, Brisk, or Physically Gifted with Trance

While mesmerizing can be utilized for execution upgrades, it can't make people more grounded or more athletic than their physical abilities.

Myth 6. Everyone Can Be Entranced

It is beyond the realm of imagination to expect to entrance everybody. One research shows that it is amazingly hypnotizable to around 10 percent of the populace. While it might be attainable to spellbind the rest of the masses, they are more reluctant to be open to the activity.

Myth 7. You Are Responsible for Your Body during Trance

Despite what you see with stage trance, you will remain aware of what you are doing and what you are being mentioned. On the off chance that you would prefer not to do anything under mesmerizing, you're not going to do it.

Myth 8. Hypnosis Is Equivalent to Rest

You may look like resting, yet during mesmerizing, you are alert. You're just in a condition of profound unwinding. Your muscles will get limp, your breathing rate will back off, and you may get sleepy.

Myth 9. When Mesmerized, Individuals Can't Lie

Sleep induction isn't a truth serum in the real world. Even though you are progressively open to a recommendation during subliminal therapy, regardless, you have through and through freedom and good judgment. Nobody can make you state anything you would prefer not to say—lie or not.

Myth 10. Many Cell Phone Applications and Web Recordings Empower Self-Trance, yet They Are Likely Inadequate

Analysts in a 2013 survey found that such instruments are not ordinarily created by an authorized trance inducer or mesmerizing association. Specialists and subliminal specialists consequently prescribe against utilizing these.

Most likely, a myth: entrancing can help you "find" lost recollections.

Even though recollections can be recouped during mesmerizing, while in a daze like a state, you might be bound to create false recollections; along these lines, numerous trance specialists remain distrustful about memory recovery utilizing spellbinding.

The primary concern entrancing holds the stage execution generalizations, alongside clacking chickens and influential artists.

As it may, Trance is a genuine remedial instrument and can be utilized for a few conditions as an elective restorative treatment. This includes the administration of a sleeping disorder, grief, and agony.

You utilize a trance specialist or subliminal specialist authorized to confide in the technique for guided trance. An organized arrangement will be made to help you accomplish your individual goals.

Chapter 24.   How Hypnosis Helps Improve Self-Esteem and Confidence

You've learned most things in your life through the unconscious, for example, how to walk and talk. Likewise, you discovered that you had to behave in a certain way even when you disagreed, or it meant that you lost your rights. Perhaps as a kid, they gave you a sweater that you didn't like as a present, and your parents forced you to put it on and show a good face with which your self-esteem started to drop, or something similar happened that slowly decreased your self-esteem.

Hypnosis working directly with the unconscious mind will help you change the values you have developed and are not sure of now. Beliefs that no longer work for you and that, with confidence and self-motivation, keep you from being a safe person.

The Relationship of Self-Esteem with the Unconscious Mind

The unconscious mind controls quite a bit about how we feel about ourselves. Our unconscious thoughts may be our best friends, or it may be our greatest critic. These thoughts are automatic and have firm roots in our minds. It may be that you look in the mirror, and your mind tells you that you don't like yourself. That low self-esteem may be the result of programming that does not help us. Our automatic thoughts are usually recorded in our brain in childhood due to the experiences we have lived and how we have interpreted them.

When you want to use hypnosis to improve self-esteem and increase your confidence, it is because those experiences have not been very positive. Now, what if you could eliminate or change these kinds of thoughts entirely? Or even something much better, what if our minds could interpret them more positively? That is the basis of hypnosis to increase self-esteem and confidence. Using clinical hypnosis, we can access these unconscious and automatic thoughts. And through the power of suggestion, we can begin to take them apart and rethink them.

Simply put, hypnosis can be a potent tool to attack the root cause of low self-esteem. Trauma can also have a significant impact on our self-esteem and self-confidence. Traumatic experiences can decrease our feelings of self-esteem and our sense of confidence.

Finally, self-esteem is presented on a scale, while others may have difficulties in certain situations.

But people with low self-esteem tend to feel a constant level of low self-esteem. They are likely to experience and feel:

- Hopelessness or depression

- Boredom or lack of motivation.

- Being overly sensitive to criticism.

- Lack of assertiveness

- Listen to a cynical and excessively critical internal dialogue

- Feeling like your life is a failure

Low Self-Esteem and Self-Confidence: Can Hypnosis Help You?

The words self-esteem and self-confidence are often used to talk about the same thing, but they are two very different ideas:

Trust can be considered as the internal judgment we make about our abilities or qualities. Therefore, I am a confident public speaker. Self-confidence can change depending on the situation. That self-confident person before a public speech could be a nervous mess singing at karaoke, and it is a measure of our feelings of self-esteem and self-love. If you have low self-esteem, either in public speaking or singing at karaoke, you have negative emotions.

What causes you to have low self-esteem or weak confidence in certain things? Self-esteem and confidence are made up of past experiences. Throughout life, we receive many negative and positive messages, which can have an impact on how we feel about ourselves.

These messages can come from our family, friends, teachers, or even from the media. And unfortunately, we are more receptive to negative messages because emotionally, they are more robust.

Neuroscience has discovered that all the experiences we live are recorded in our brains, creating a neural path of behavior. Depending on the degree of emotional intensity or the experience's repetition, that "neural path" or behavior may have more influence on our behavior than another. Because negative emotions tend to be more powerful, negative beliefs may have a more significant effect on our behavior than positive ones.

You Can Improve Your Self-Esteem

- There is hope. You can fix negative thinking patterns in your mind.

- In fact, low self-esteem is a lot like a technical problem in your mind.

- But self-esteem is flexible.

- At different periods of our lives, it can be high or low. We can learn to improve it or make adjustments.

- In other words, we are not condemned to lives of low self-esteem.

Hypnosis to increase Self-Esteem and Confidence

Self-esteem has a decisive influence on everything you do and how you feel. It is the subjective assessment that we have about ourselves as human beings. What we believe about the kind of person we are, our abilities, and what we hope to be in the future. What we feel about ourselves in the present.

Self-esteem is a fully learned personal characteristic, and it is not a birth trait like height or eye color. The experiences and the conclusions drawn from those experiences determine the perception that one has of oneself.

"What disturbs people is not things but the impressions they have of them" Epictetus.

Issues related to self-esteem usually originate in childhood. Our personal history and relationships with the people around us, parents, siblings, and friends, give rise to our opinion of ourselves.

We receive all kinds of messages as we grow, affirmative and negative. But for some reason, most humans tend to pay more attention and stick with the negative. Feelings of not being good enough can continue to affect us in our adult lives.

Another possible source of low self-esteem, especially among young people, is the media's enormous pressure. We are constantly bombarded with images and stories of successful people, a fragmented and unreal vision. Comparing yourself to these people and feeling unsuccessful and worthless is easy if you don't have the right psychological mechanisms. Good self-esteem is the foundation.

Finally, traumatic events, verbal or physical abuse can affect self-esteem. Being subjected to unpleasant circumstances against our will often cause us to lose confidence in others and ourselves. We often feel responsible and guilty for things that we have no control over. The image of ourselves, self-esteem, is affected.

Each person is different, and low self-esteem affects people in different ways. If a person feels worthless and worthless, his behavior influenced, confirming this vision of himself. Then you have a series of thoughts and feelings that a person with low self-esteem may experience:

- Negative thoughts about yourself

- Lack of confidence and security

- Feelings of permanent uncertainty and hesitation

- Lack of motivation

- The sense of constant failure

- Feelings of inferiority

- Feelings of being useless, hopeless, and depressed

- Feelings of boredom

- Feelings of anxiety and worry permanently about making a mistake

- Feelings of vulnerability to any criticism

- Thoughts that nothing has a solution and lack of expectations

- Lack of assertiveness

- Feeling tired and lack of energy

- Constant wishes for a better life

The most severe thing is that all these series of difficulties have repercussions in the lives of people who experience low self-esteem. People who struggle with low self-esteem seek the approval of others. They try to reaffirm themselves by observing the reactions and comments of those around them to value themselves.

Overcoming low self-esteem means learning to accept yourself according to your criteria without waiting for the assessment of other people.

Chapter 25.   Tips and Tricks

To achieve your weight loss goals, you must be willing to let in any fear and doubt about hypnotherapy. It is not something that you can second guess, particularly not its effectivity and results-driven orientation. It is a solution used for many different reasons, even other than weight loss. Hypnotherapy for weight loss can help you overcome a negative relationship with food, one that may have formed over a period or throughout your entire life. It is something that can present you with proper results and that you can always be sure of.

Although it is not a diet or weight loss supplement, it fulfills a similar supporting role and serves as the foundation for a more mindful lifestyle. Since the method thereof focuses on replacing old negative habits with new positive ones, it helps overcome challenges faced when trying to lose weight.

Both can serve you usefully whether you want to opt for a one-on-one weight loss for hypnotherapy session or listen to audiobooks online.

Before you dive into the world of hypnotherapy, you should know that there's a lot more to it than you initially thought. Much like Yoga and meditation, in general, it serves a higher purpose as it leads you on to a mindful path of physical, mental, and emotional wellness.

Tips for Hypnosis for Weight Loss

Find the Right Hypnotherapist for Weight Loss for You

How would you go about doing this, you may ask? Instead of going the obvious route of searching for hypnotherapists online in your area, why not ask for recommendations instead? What's better than asking a friend, family member, or acquaintance to recommend you an ethical hypnotherapist for weight loss? If no one knows or knows a hypnotherapist known for the outstanding jobs they perform, you may want to check with your doctor and ask for advice. They should be able to recommend a qualified and results-oriented hypnotherapist for weight loss. To ensure you have the right hypnotherapist once you have found one, check with yourself to see if your consultation felt like it was thorough—if the hypnotherapy program was adjusted to meet your needs, if the practitioner was helpful and answered all your questions. When hypnotherapists allow space between sessions, it is also an indication that you are dealing with an ethical hypnotherapist.

Don't Pay Any Attention to Advertising

We live in 2019, which means that everything we see online is taken seriously. However, it shouldn't be. People are oblivious and susceptible to accept everything they read or hear, but not everything can be trusted when it comes to advertising. Advertising should, ever so often, be disregarded and not taken too seriously as it can be very misleading. It's always better to conduct your research before you accept that something is a sure way or not. In the case of hypnotherapy, since there are so many negative associations related to the practice, it's best to find out what's it all about yourself. As you can see from this useful set of information about hypnotherapy for weight loss, it is entirely safe and probably nothing negative that you expected it to be.

Get Information about Training, Qualifications, and Necessary Experience

Before you pick a hypnotherapist, you must be sure about their essential information first. Do they run their practice or operate independently? Are they certified and have a license? Ensuring that they also adhere to ethical standards, most preferably recommended by other medical physicians, you'll be assured that you are dealing with someone who knows what they are doing.

Before Choosing One Hypnotherapist, Talk to Several First

Perhaps one of the best ways to find out whether a hypnotherapist is best suited for you is to speak with a few of them over a phone call first. This will take some effort, but it will be worth it in the end. You have to consider whether they can relate to you, care about your well-being, and listen to your concerns, whether they are personable, accommodating, and professional. If they tick all the boxes, then you're good to go.

Don't Fall For Any Promises That May Sound Unrealistic

If a hypnotist tells you that their therapy session will help you lose weight fast, don't even bother going to a single session. In reality, hypnosis for weight loss is a process that takes time. It can take anywhere between three weeks up to three months to see your physical body change and lose weight. Since your body and mind should first adjust, you need to allow time to do so. Hypnosis for weight loss isn't a fad, nor is it a means of losing weight overnight. It's also essential to avoid hypnotherapists who suggest they will make you lose weight. Since they will only talk during the session, what they are telling you is not true at all, which you can expect from a professional and authentic hypnotherapist; however, a professional individual takes responsibility for helping you get where you want to go. This person should help you access your subconscious mind with ease and help you bring it on board with a proper weight loss plan and possibly an exercise routine.

Is Your Hypnotherapist of Choice Multi-Skilled?

Hypnosis is a terrific tool and can alter the mind's way of thinking about food, and it goes hand-in-hand with nutrition. This is something you need to consider, mainly whether your hypnotist has a good understanding of what it takes for you to lose weight sustainably and healthily. Many people who are focused on starting a weight loss journey don't necessarily know what to do or what they should eat. When looking for a hypnotherapist, look for self-help coaching or some psychotherapy qualification and a qualification/background in either nutrition or cognitive behavioral therapy.

Find Out the Time You Should Engage in a Program

This is quite important as hypnotherapy can become quite expensive if you're going to a professional for one-on-one sessions. If you prefer going to a professional rather than conducting the courses at your home, you can choose to spread your sessions over time to make it more affordable. Even though you may think that the meetings become less useful to achieve the overall effect, it works more effectively as your mind and body require time to adjust. Time is also needed as you change your old habits and replace them with new ones.

Ask Your Hypnotherapist if They Can Provide You with a Program to Maintain Your Progress at Home

A recording mainly helps to allow you to spread out sessions over time. Listening to your weight loss hypnosis recording will keep you in check and help you stay motivated and focused.

As Your Hypnotherapist, if They Can Tailor-Make Your Hypnotherapy Weight Loss Program for You

If they agree to it, you can expect a weight loss hypnotherapy program that is much more effective than individualized hypnosis. It offers treatments that may work better than ones that cater to everyone. Since every person is different compared to others, this makes a lot more sense. Sure, the general program will work, but a personalized one could offer you better results.

Ask Whether Your Program Includes an Introduction Session

Starting with hypnotherapy for weight loss, you don't want to dive right into it. It's essential to take the necessary time, even if it's just an hour, to establish your needs and concerns regarding your current habits, lifestyle, and goals with your hypnotherapist. Ensuring that they care about your well-being and results instead of just taking you through the session is equally important. Taking the time to talk to your hypnotherapist and getting to know them better will help you feel more at ease and form a foundation of trust before starting your hypnotherapy sessions.

Establish the Costs Involved Before Starting with Your Sessions

Ensuring you know how much an initial consultation and each session fee will be another essential factor you have to consider before choosing a hypnotherapist. Considering the cost, consider an overview of your program in comparison to other potential weight loss programs. Review the price only in terms of the quality of service you will receive and keep in mind that you can spread your request over weeks rather than going to a few sessions a week.

Lastly, it would help if you viewed hypnotherapy as an investment in yourself and well-being rather than an unnecessary expense. The context for this thought will realize once you engage in or complete your program.

Chapter 26.   Portion Control Hypnosis

Whether you wish to shed many pounds or maintain a healthy weight, proper portion consumption is necessary to consume appropriate foods. The rate of obesity among youngsters and adults has increased partly owing to the increase in restaurant portions.

A portion is the total quantity of food that you eat in one sitting. A serving size is the suggested quantity of one food. For instance, the amount of steak you eat for dinner maybe a portion; however, three ounces of steak, maybe a serving. Controlling serving sizes helps with portion control.

Health Benefits of Portion Control

Serious health problems are caused by overeating—for example, type 2 diabetes, weight problems, high blood pressure, and many more. Therefore, portion control should be a significant priority when you are looking to lead a healthy lifestyle.

Fullness and Weight Management

Feeling satiable, or having a sense of fullness, will affect the quantity you eat and the way you usually eat. According to the British Nutrition Foundation, eating smaller portions slowly increases the feeling of satiety after a meal.

Eating smaller parts also permits your body to use the food you eat right away for energy, rather than storing the excess as fat. Losing weight is not as straightforward as solely controlling your portion sizes; however, once you learn to observe the quantity of food you eat, you will begin to apply conscious intake, which might assist you in making healthier food decisions.

When you eat too quickly, you do not notice your stomach's cues that it is full. Eat slowly and listen to hunger cues to enhance feelings of fullness and, ultimately, consume less food.

Improved Digestion

Considerably larger portion sizes contribute to an upset stomach and discomfort (caused by a distended stomach pushing down on your other organs). Your gastrointestinal system functions best when it is not full of food. Managing portions can help to get rid of cramping and bloating after eating. Furthermore, you may run into the danger of getting pyrosis because having a full abdomen will push hydrochloric acid back into your digestive tract.

Money Savings

Eating smaller parts may lead to monetary benefits, mainly when eating out. In addition to eating controlled serving sizes, you do not have to purchase as many groceries. Measuring serving proportions can make the box of cereal and packet of nuts last longer than eating straight out of the container.

For instance, the method to apply portion management at restaurants is to order kid-sized meals that are typically cheaper than adult meals and closer to the right serving size you ought to be eating.

Adult portion sizes at restaurants will equal two, three, or even more servings. Therefore, immediately the food arrives at your table, request a takeaway container and put away half of your food from the plate. Take your food home, and this way, you will have two meals for one's worth.

How to Control Portions Using Hypnosis

Hypnosis can take you into a deeply relaxed state and quickly train your mind to understand when to do away with excess food instinctively and allow your digestion to be lighter and more comfortable. You may discover the pleasure of being in tune with what your own body requires nourishment. Hypnosis will re-educate your instincts to regulate hunger pangs. As you relax and repeatedly listen to powerful hypnotic suggestions that are going to be absorbed by your mind; you may quickly begin to note that:

- Your mind is no longer engrossed in food

- Your abdomen and gut feel lighter

- You now do not feel uncontrollable hunger pangs at 'non-meal' times

- You naturally forget to have food between meals

- You begin to enjoy a healthier lifestyle

There is a somewhat simple self-hypnosis process for helping you control your appetite and portions. In a shell, you are immersing yourself into a psychological state and picture a dial or a flip switch of some type that is symbolic of your craving and your real hunger. Then you repeatedly apply to develop a true sense of control, then you employ it out of the hypnotic state and when confronted with those things and circumstances to curb the perceived hunger and control your appetite.

Step 1

Get yourself into a comfortable position and one where you will remain undisturbed for the period of this exercise. Ascertain your feet are flat on the ground and hands not touching. Then once you are in position, calm yourself.

You can do that by using hypnosis tapes; they are basic processes to assist you in opening the door of your mind.

Step 2

You may prefer to deepen your hypnotic state. The best and most straightforward is imagining yourself in your favorite place and relaxing your body bit by bit. Keep focused on the session at hand (that is, watch out not to drift off), then go to the third step.

Step 3

Take a picture of a dial, a lever, or a flippy switch of some kind on a box or mounted on a wall of some sort-let that fully controls your mind's eye. Notice the colors, the materials that it is created out of, and the way it indicates 0-10 to mark the variable degrees of your real hunger.

Notice wherever it is indicating currently; let it show you how hungry you are. Remember when last you ate, what you ate, whether the hunger is genuine or merely reacting to a recent bout of gluttony and wanting to gratify that sensation!

Once you have established the dial, where it is set, and trust that the reading is correct, then go to the subsequent step.

Step 4

Flip the dial down a peg and notice the effects taking place within you. Study your feedback and ascertain that it feels like you are moving your appetite with the dial. The more you believe you are affecting your appetite with the dial, the more practical its application in those real-life situations.

Practice turning it down even lower and start recognizing how you use your mind to change your perceived appetite utilizing a healthy method and helps keep you alert when you encounter circumstances with plenty of food supply. Tell yourself that the more you observe this, the better control you gain over your appetite.

You might even create a strong affirmation that accompanies this dial "I am in control of my eating" is one such straightforward statement. Word it as you wish and make sure it is one thing that resonates well with you. Once you have repeated the meaningful affirmations to yourself severally with conviction, proceed to the following step.

Step 5

Visualize yourself during a future scenario, where there is going to be constant temptation to continue eating although you are full or to consume an excessive amount. See the sights of that place, take a mental note of the other people there, notice the smells, and hear the sounds. Become increasingly aware of how you are feeling in this place. Get the most definition and clarity possible, and then notice that you turn down the dial on your craving once the temptation presents itself. You realize that you are not hungry to eat anymore, then repeat your positive affirmations to yourself a few more times to strengthen it.

Run through this future situation severally on loop to make sure your mind is mentally rehearsed about your plan to respond.

Step 6

Twitch your little finger and toes, then open your eyes and proceed to observe your skills in real-life and spot how much control you have.

Chapter 27.   Banning Food

The entire intuitive eating approach revolves around listening to the body and keeping a finger on its pulse. If you are unable to follow the signals your body is giving out properly, you will face problems in implementing this lifestyle. Any dietician that you go to initially or talk about with on the subject of intuitive eating will tell you that it's based on recognizing hunger and satisfying the needs accordingly. Earlier on, you read how there are different kinds of desire, and what you feel at times is not always what it seems like. Most of us are only familiar with physical hunger and spend our lives believing that it's the only type that exists.

The healthy living approach of intuitive eating has informed us that this is not the case. Your body experiences varying forms of hunger, and you do not always have to be satisfied with the consumption of food. One of the first core principles of this philosophy teaches people to honor their hunger. This is about being aware of the biological urge which asks you to eat and then stop when you no longer feel empty. People say that this can get confusing at times as, during the initial stages, they are still trying to train their body and mind. If you think about it, exploring where and what kind of hunger may not be as difficult as one would assume.

There are no technicalities or complications that you have to unravel. Just consider these few points:

- When you feel hungry, wherein can your body handle the physical sensation? Are your stomach-wrenching and gnawing? If not, does your throat itch for something? Do you feel sluggish and tired? Sometimes, you might not experience any such thing but instead start feeling weak and experiencing a headache. If this happens out of nowhere, it's a sign that your body needs to be replenished with nutrients.

- Does hunger affect your mood or concentration? Do you find yourself thinking of food in the middle of work or a conversation? Those who have answered yes to both these questions, well, there you have it. When you feel hungry, your mood changes for the worse, your ability to concentrate on any task hinders, and if your thoughts are going out to meals and snacks, then that is quite obvious.

- Are there any changes in your hunger when you travel, stressed, or functioning on low sleep? To determine those, you need to closely monitor your body and try to remedy the change source because a disturbance in the eating pattern may be emotional hunger rather than physical.

An integral aspect here which people should be mindful of is that everyone experiences or feels hunger differently, and what one person goes through does not apply to the other. Just remember that intuitive eating has no wrong answers, and it's a practice that brings about gradual progress, so if you do not get it instantly, there is nothing wrong with that because no one ever does.

Moving on to the other hunger, which we talked about that is emotional and does not require any satisfaction, which comes from food. People generally experience four types of desire: real, which you should immediately respond to according to the intuitive eating philosophy, and then emotional, practical, and taste. In the beginning, you found out what physical and emotional hunger was about and how to successfully deal with each of them. Physical hunger is perhaps the most important one here as it's your body reaching out to you and sending cues. This is also something that a lot of people fail to pay adequate attention to. You see, the diet mentality and culture has led to many treating their necessary hunger as an enemy. They consider it a challenge that has to be overcome because it would result in shame and guilt. Well, how can something so essential and necessary for your survival be wrong for you? Hence, when your body begins to communicate with you, learn to listen.

Chapter 28. Consider Incorporating Working Out into Your Routine

The Rules of Working Out

That said, when you get going on a new exercise regimen, there are a few things you can keep in mind. These will help you get started and make sure you get the right kind of workout to suit your needs.

Firstly, the type of exercise you select will make a huge difference. To target your whole body, you need to be able to pick out a wide range of workouts. Cardio is the first form, and you should spend three to four days a week getting some of this into your routine as it increases your heart rate and makes sure your heart gets some of the treatment it needs. Plus, the weight loss is really great because you can burn a lot of calories in the process.

That doesn't mean certain forms of workouts aren't important. Weight lifting can also be done a couple of days a week because it also strengthens those muscles. Your metabolism will burn much faster during the day while doing normal activities when the muscles are toned up. So, while you may not burn as many calories as you do with cardio during the actual workout part, weight lifting can be amazing for the metabolism benefits.

And on stretching, you can't forget; take some time off your days, and do some stretching, like yoga or some other technique. This can help give the muscles a good time to relax after working so hard during the week, making them stronger and leaner and preventing injury.

Now, when it comes to how long you're supposed to work out, that will vary. When you want to lose weight, it's recommended you work out at least three days a week for 45 to 60 minutes. However, some people prefer to work out at whatever minutes for five or six days, so it's easier to fit into their schedule. When you are just beginning your fitness routine, and it's been a while since you've worked out, starting slow is best. Ten minutes is better than nothing, and from there, you can build up. Never say you don't have time to work out; you can fit three or four ten-minute sessions into the day, and you've completed a full workout once you've done it.

Make sure the workouts you select have a lot of variety. Mix the stretching, cardio, and weight-lifting days together. Test out a host of different things, including some you've never done before. Mixing it up helps to focus on various muscle groups that help with weight loss and make your workout easier to enjoy.

What if I Don't Have Time to Work Out?

Some people worry they wouldn't have time to work out. They imagine spending hours at the gym to get the extra exercise they need to really see the results they like. Yet you don't need to waste all this time in the gym with a successful weight loss program. You just need to work out a few days a week and then find other ways to fit into your routine a little bit of exercise. Some of the easy ways you can add to your routine in more movement include: get up every hour, rather than sitting at your desk all day long and never moving, consider getting up every hour for at least two to five minutes. Walk around the room, do some jumping jacks and run around just a bit. For five minutes of an eight-hour day every hour, you'll end up for forty-five minutes of exercise. You should bring this around too. Do some sit-ups and pushups during commercial breaks during your favorite show, and you will get an additional fifteen to twenty minutes each hour.

Park further away—if you need to take your vehicle, make sure you park far from the entrance. It might be just a few extra measures, but you do it a few times a day, and it really adds up.

Working Out During Your Lunch

Working out during your lunch break can be one of the best choices you can make. You can spend your lunch break just twenty minutes and then enjoy a nutritious meal for the rest. This won't take too much of your time, so it can be a nice way to stroll around the office or work in the local gym without adjusting your schedule too much.

Take the Stairs

If you're working in an office just below the first floor, try going up the stairs instead of the elevator. If the office is too far up to walk, start with a few flights and then take the rest of the way up the elevator. With time, you'll be able to increase your endurance and go up more flights of stairs.

Learn Chair Exercises

If you can't get up from your chair at work too often, learn a few basic exercises that will help you to work out your body without moving too often.

Add Moves to Chores

Just cleaning the house can make you all sweaty. Make the movement intentional and add some things to it, and you're sure you'll get the additional exercise you want while making the house look fine.

Play at the park—take your kids to the park (walk there if you can) and then play at the park. Using the monkey bars, ride them, go down the slides, and more. You'll be shocked to see how much of a workout this will end up for you.

There's still time to add more exercise to your day; for that to happen, you just need to be a little creative. If you get up more often from your chair or sneak a few times during the day in the workouts, you're sure to get the results you want.

The Benefits of Working Out

There are plenty of perks you'll reap when it comes to working out. You'll see a huge difference in the way your body behaves and responds, you'll be able to lower your stress levels, and your attitude will begin to feel better in no time. Only ten minutes a day will make a major difference in the overall way you feel. Some of the great benefits you'll be able to see when you start working out include:

Better Mood

It's time to have a workout on those days when you're just mad at everyone and grumpy... Even if you feel down and down, it's time to get out there and enjoy a good workout. Ten to fifteen minutes is all you need to make your mood feel better, and if you can work out for longer, you'll find that your body feels so much happier and satisfied when it's over.

Clearer Mind

There's just something to figure out that will clean the mind out and make you feel so much better. When you feel foggy or can't get any more work done for the day and only lunchtime, think about going out there and going into a good workout.

Healthier Heart

Your heart still wants some exercise. At least a few times a day, you want to use cardio to help the heart get up there and get stronger. Also, if you have to start slowly, you will find in the beginning that working your heart with some good workouts like walking, running, swimming, and cycling will help you get that heart in shape.

Faster Weight Loss

You eat calories while you work out. So, the more calories you eat up, the faster the weight loss becomes. Your metabolism should be quicker, and it can eat up all the fat excess that remains in the body, so you'll be able to see some of those weight loss results quicker than ever before.

Toned Muscles

Sitting on the couch doesn't help your muscles be safe and strong. Instead, it makes them frail and fragile and wastes them away. Neither do you just have to focus on weight lifting; stretching and cardio also have those muscles up and going, and you can see more strength in your body. Besides, these toned muscles will help speed up the metabolism, which is good whether you choose to lose weight or not.

Leaves You Wanting More

Beginning on an exercise plan may seem difficult at the beginning, and you may want to go out and do something else; you will learn to love it. If you can only keep up with the job for some time, you can see some amazing results in the process. You'll start looking forward to the workout, for instance, to see how many results you can achieve. If you're someone who gets bored with the workout, just have a plan every few months or so to change it, and you're going to be perfect.

Although many people hate working out and putting all the time into it, there is actually a lot of good from daily exercise. Give it a chance together with the other parts of your Successful weight loss program plan to see how much the outcomes will improve.

Chapter 29.   Your Thinner and Happier Life

Benefits of Eating Healthy and Detoxifying

Most times, we don't eat because we are hungry; we eat because food is available. The same way you make arbitrary decisions to purchase items you don't need in a supermarket in the same way you purchase food. Most times, when you get a job that offers you some financial freedom, you begin to go to that expensive restaurant you have dreamt of going because you can now afford it.

Now that you can afford the food there, you frequently visit the restaurant and purchase food you do not need. You are just buying the food because you have the money to do so, and the food is readily available. Many of the bad decisions that make us eat food that we do not need to eat can be avoided if we start to focus our thoughts on getting what is necessary.

The process of getting what is necessary requires you as an individual to be able to acquire some personal discipline. Before you purchase any food, you need to ask yourself if buying the diet is necessary. Ask yourself if the food that you are eating will add any value to your overall health. After asking yourself that question, you know the right thing to do, based on the questions' response. It is a natural process to do, and it will help save you from eating those carbs that only add unnecessary weight to your body.

Maintain a Healthy Body

Once we consume food, our bodies respond to what we have consumed. The response could be negative or positive. Different foods generate different feelings. You may not believe what some of these feelings are, except you focus your minds on realizing them. The power of meditation is that it allows you to focus and concentrate on something that requires your attention. This is an easy task to accomplish, and you only should evaluate how your body reacts to the foods you are consuming. Once you eat some foods, you will notice that you feel energized, while some foods will make you feel tired.

Once you overeat, you will experience some sudden feelings of tiredness. You will begin to feel as if your body is too heavy, and so all you want to do is take a nap or a rest. Now when this happens, you should realize that it is a sign that whatever you ate was unnecessary, and hence the body will not use the food. As a result, most of what you ate will become something that your body needs to eliminate. Thus, you will start to add extra weight because your body's excess food becomes excess fat in your body. On the other hand, if you eat, it immediately makes you feel energized; it means your body was receptive to your food.

It means that your body was able to convert much of the food into energy, and your body will well utilize each of that component present in the diet. This is beneficial for your body's wellbeing, and it can help you when losing weight and prevent you from adding unnecessary weight.

Maintain the Bodyweight

Your eyes are shut. Envision coasting your desires ceaselessly. Envision what's pleasant for you to eat a day. Envision spellbinding, helping you get in shape as the news seems to be. Psychotherapist Jean Fain from the

Harvard Medical School gives ten trancelike recommendations to endeavor.

When I tell people how I make a lot of my life—as a psychotherapist who entrances thin individuals—they ask: Does that work? Typically, my reaction lights up their eyes with something among energy and unbelief.

A great many people don't comprehend that adding daze to your weight reduction endeavors can enable you to lose more weight and look after it. Spellbinding originates before the tallying of carb and calories by a few decades. However, this well-established technique for centering consideration presently can't be held entirely onto a practical weight reduction methodology.

As of not long ago, the real claims of prestigious trance inducers have bolstered by insufficient logical proof, and an excess of pie-in-the-sky responsibilities from their issue kin, stage trance specialists, have not made a difference.

Indeed, even after a powerful reanalysis of 18 sleep-inducing studies in the mid-1990s demonstrated that psychotherapy clients who appropriately self-trance lost twice as much weight as compared to the individuals who didn't (and held it off in one research two years after the part of the bargain) unless if you or somebody you know has joyfully been constrained by entrancing to buy a crisp, littler closet. It might be hard to believe that this psyche over-body procedure can enable you to take a few to get back some composure on eating.

Seeing is thinking absolutely. So, investigate yourself. To gain proficiency with a portion of the priceless exercises that trance must instruct about weight reduction, you don't need to be spellbound. The ten smaller than expected ideas that pursue contain a portion of the eating regimen modifying recommendations that my gathering and individual hypnotherapy weight the executive's clients get.

The power is inside. Trance specialists believe that you have all you should be useful. You truly needn't bother with the other accident diet or the ongoing suppressant of hunger. When you ride a bike, thinning is tied in with confiding in your innate abilities. You may not recall how terrifying it was that you previously endeavored to ride a bike. However, you kept on rehearsing until you had the option to ride, consequently, with no idea or exertion. Getting more fit may appear past you moreover. However, it's just about finding your balance.

You see your conviction. Individuals will, in general, do what they accept they can achieve. That is even valid for mesmerizing. Those fooled into deduction could be entranced (for example, as the trance inducer proposed they would see red, he turned the switch on a disguised red bulb), demonstrating improved mesmerizing reaction. It is essential to hope to be made a difference. Give me a chance to propose you anticipate that your arrangement should work on weight reduction. Highlight the positive. Recommendations, for example, "Doughnuts will sicken you," negative or aversive, work for some time, however on the off chance that you need lasting change, you need to think definitely. Specialists Herbert Spiegel and David Spiegel, a dad child hypnotherapy group, considered the most well-known valuable trancelike proposition. "I need my body to live in. I owe regard and security to my body." I elevate clients to create their very own energetic mantras. A 50-year-old mother who shed 50 pounds more rehashes day by day: "Superfluous nourishment is a weight on my body. I will shed what I needn't bother with."

It's going to come if you envision it. Like competitors who are getting ready for the challenge, you are set up for a victorious truth by picturing triumph. Envisioning a smart dieting day will enable you to envision the means expected to turn into a decent eater. Is it too difficult to even think about photographing? Locate a comfortable old photograph of yourself and recall what you did another way. Envision these schedules reviving. Or, on the other hand, picture acquiring direction from a more former, more astute self later on in the wake of contacting her required weight.

Get Rid of Cravings

Subliminal specialists utilize the intensity of typical symbolism on a standard premise, welcoming subjects to put sustenance desires on fleecy white mists or inflatables in sight-seeing and send them up, up, and away. On the off chance that you can direct off your eating routine from McDonald's brilliant curves, trance inducers comprehend that a counter-image can control you back. Welcome your psyche to flip through its picture Rolodex until you develop as an indication of yearnings throwing out. Push.

There are two preferred procedures over one. A triumphant mix is entrancing and Cognitive Behavioral Treatment (CBT) with regards to getting more fit and holding it off, which patches up counterproductive thoughts and practices. Clients learning both lose twice as much weight without falling into lose a few and recuperate more health food nut. On the off chance that you've kept up a sustenance journal, you've officially endeavored CBT. They monitor everything that experiences their lips for possibly 14 days before my clients learn mesmerizing. Each great trance inducer comprehends that raising cognizance is a principle move for the tyke towards suffering change.

Modify and Then Change

The late pioneer of the spell, Milton Erickson, MD, focused on one's core. To improve loss-recovery, taking a cue from one client, Erickson recommended that you gain weight before you lose weight, a hard sell today, except if you're Charlize Theron. Easier to swallow: modify your high-calorie craving. Shouldn't something be said about a solidified yogurt instead of 16 ounces of dessert?

Like it or not, it is the fittest for survival. No proposal is sufficiently able to supersede the nature of survival. Similarly, as we like to believe, it's the most appropriate survival, despite everything we're modified for durability in case of starvation. A valid example: a private dietary mentor needed a proposal for her dependence on a sticky bear. The adviser attempted to clarify that her body felt that her life relied upon the chewy desserts and wouldn't surrender until she got enough calories from progressively nutritious food. No, she demanded; all that she required was a proposition when she dropped out.

Practice Makes Perfect

There are no washboard abs that one Pilate's class delivers, and one spellbinding session can't shape your eating routine. Be that as it may, discreetly rehashing a useful suggestion 15 to 20 minutes daily can change your eating, especially when combined with moderate, regular breaths, the foundation of any social change program.

Chapter 30.   The Final Weight Loss Puzzle

We can all be thin when we choose to, but most of us have been brain-washed with weight-loss companies and diets that we tend to ignore our bodies instead of following medical establishments blindly. Our bodies are also wiser than several varieties of nutrition in the market. However, with diverse information reporting to us how unhealthy foods will affect our weights, we have turned deaf ears on what the body is communicating.

The secret to becoming naturally thin is to follow the four basic rules of life. The rules will guide you on when to eat, how to eat, what to eat, and how much you need to eat to avoid weight gain. These habits will enable you to eat whatever you crave and ensure that you have the healthiest body.

Eat Only When You Are Hungry

When you choose to starve your body, you might begin to lose weight but only for a short period. The body will react immediately by slowing down the metabolism process to ensure that enough fats are stored for the organization. This is usually aimed at allowing the body to survive for a more extended period until it refeeds.

As soon as you begin eating, the boy will naturally store up all the food to prepare for the next starvation. This means that when you continuously eat after a period of starving, all the food will be stored in the form of fats, thereby resulting in weight gain.

Additionally, some people may find themselves overeating once they move beyond a period of starvation. The body is usually hungry, and it is always difficult to control how much one eats, causing an influx in the number of calories that the body can contain. In such a case, you may find yourself gaining back all the weight you gained during starvation but also end up winning even more.

So, the bottom line is when you are hungry, you should EAT without hesitation.

Stop Eating When You Are Full

Another important step towards attaining a slim body is always to stop eating when you feel full.

One of the ways to know when you are full is to put your spoon or fork down between your bites. The automatic cycle of hand-to-mouth as people eat may cause overfeeding. Once you take a bit, give your spoon or fork rest to tune into your body's cues. You will be able to tell when you are full and satisfied.

An important tip to always stop eating when feeling full is turning off any distractions while eating. Studies have shown that people tend to eat 14 times more when they watch TV. This is associated with a lack of mindful eating that makes us unable to control our food intake.

Eat Only What You Crave

With the ongoing love-hate relationship we have with food, eating what you want, not what you think you should, sounds like a fabulous piece of cake. We often forget that eating is one of life's simplest pleasures. Deprivation of certain foods makes them all the more attractive to you. Eating what you want creates a balanced relationship with all fares. Most diabetics, when asked, what food they miss the most are those restricted by the doctors, that is, salts, sugar (sweetened food), and white grubs. This is because their relationship with these foods created a tension that upset the balance. Listening to your body releases you from the guilt and anxiety that come from not following a strict dietary plan.

Enjoying food is essential because then you can listen to it when you have had enough. Provided you are hungry, and you are free to eat whatever you want and thoroughly enjoy it. Trust your gut because you are no longer what you eat but why you eat. The reasons you eat make a world of difference in informing your meal decisions, when to eat, what to eat, and when to stop. A few elements make food pleasurable: smell, taste, temperature, substance, presentation, and texture. When you crave a cheesy, warm, savory meal, a crispy, cold salad will not do the trick. You will not receive the same satisfaction from it as much as you expected with the warm meal.

Denying yourself foods you like often leads to over-eating when you get the chance to eat them, as well as the foods you are currently "permitted" to eat. The reason for this is because you wind up looking for satisfaction elsewhere—the pleasure you expect to feel with certain foods not easily substituted with different foods. Additionally, you do not like eating meals would lead you to eat quickly to finish, which is not necessarily responsible. Eating slowly helps you listen to when you become full.

When you enjoy your food, the following happens:

- You digest your food better. Your gastrointestinal system relaxes, releasing more digestive juices. When you eat something with guilt, your body is under stress, and that tension puts a strain on the digestive tract causing it to be that much slower and triggering gut issues like bloating.

- You will be satisfied with less.

- You absorb more nutrients. When you enjoy the food, absorption of nutrients takes effect mainly because the entire digestive tract is working at optimum capacity.

We are fully aware of our nutritional needs. Most people worry that if they always gave in to their cravings, they might never make healthy decisions. The contrary is true. Your body is always asking for different things at different times of the day and through the weeks. Any food that does not cause you pleasure should not form any part of your meal.

Eat Consciously and Enjoy Every Bite You Make

Eating consciously involves mindfulness with every food you buy, prepare, serve, and consume. Most people eat far too quickly to induce the feel-good hormone that is discharged with feelings of pleasure. Eating fast then makes you overlook the signs of satisfaction that your body is hinting at, and you end up stretching out your stomach and putting on weight. The same pleasure you chased fleetingly disappears, and the guilt takes hold. To alleviate the blame, you crave food, and the vicious cycle continues.

Mindfulness provides a balance between overeating and under eating while making you consciously aware of every bite and the sensations that accompany it. It is impossible to do something unless you know exactly what you are doing. That said, it is more important to feed your hunger than to feed your face. Unconsciously gulping down food like a barn animal brings about unwanted physical, psychological, and emotional concerns.

To reclaim your consciousness when eating:

- Start with your grocery shopping. Make sure you only purchase the foods you thoroughly enjoy.

- Exercise regular self-observation and be compassionate to yourself in case you catch yourself slipping.

- Allocate time to meals. Take about thirty minutes to an hour out of your day to sit down and enjoy your food.

- Avoid multitasking and distractions during meal times. Avoid eating in front of the fridge or the Tv. Sit down with your food as the only thing in front of you and engage your senses.

- Always serve your meal on a plate or a bowl. Avoid eating from the packaging.

- Take small bites and chew thoroughly while engaged in every mouthful

The focus would be to shift your mind from just thinking about food to taking yourself on an epicurious journey. Eating consciously leads to emotional health, along with:

- Reducing stress on the body and the mind

- Eating deliberately, according to researchers, helps you reach your optimal weight by cutting the excessive eating

- Healthy blood sugar levels

- Improved relationship with food

Exercising mindfulness in food as well as life generally leads you to do the right things properly.

Food is food. There is no "good" or "bad" (unless it is inedible), and at this point, it fails to qualify as food. When we remove the stigma associated with food cravings, we become liberated and enjoy our food experiences fully. Mindful eating might be new to Western culture, but it is a tried and tested technique in the Asian culture over a long period.

When our limiting inner dialogue on food no longer guides us, we can cultivate new thoughts based on our conscious eating- freed from the shackles of deprivation of certain food types. Our approach to food and eating experiences becomes something to which we can look forward. Awareness with food gives a pause allowing us to consider our impulses and reactions from time-to-time. To unlock mindfulness eating, ask yourself how you relate to food and be frank with yourself. It is also noteworthy to note that not all people have the same relationship dynamic with food.

Conclusion

Congratulations on getting to the end. If you have been struggling to lose weight, you don't have to anymore. With the information you have gained from here, you can now embark on your weight loss journey with boldness because you know, this time, you will succeed. You can be sure that your efforts will not go in vain, far from it. This time you will achieve your goals and progressively become the person you have always wanted to be.

Perhaps you have been yo-yo dieting, and every plan you engage in fails. By understanding the reasons, you overindulge is one of the best ways to begin this journey. Hypnotism is a great way to address any underlying issues that may be causing you to overeat and gain weight.

As we have stated multiple times, you have everything you need to be successful. So, it is now only a matter of making the most of your efforts. Furthermore, you will find that being consistent will yield the best results.

The techniques in hypnotherapy have been used for hundreds of years, and many people have reported positive results. How we do things is deeply embedded in our subconscious minds. A mind is a powerful tool, and changing your mindset about food will help you have a healthier relationship with food. Hypnosis can help you transform your account to eliminate emotional eating and lose weight.

You have also realized that apart from going to see a professional hypnotist, one can be able to self-hypnotize. You can do this to aid you in controlling the portions you eat.

At the end of it all, it is about eating consciously. Adapting mindful eating habits will help you maintain a healthy lifestyle even after reaching your goal weight. As you purpose to eat more attentively, be sure to engage a hypnotist that you can trust to take you through the journey. If you choose to self-hypnotize, you don't have to procrastinate anymore; download an app to help you and start your journey today.

Always remember calories and your consumption, as well as spending on them. Start physical exercises and control your portions to cut down on your calorie consumption. As such, this process doesn't have to be stressful. Far from it. It merely needs to be a routine that you can focus on so that it feels right for you.

As always, if you have found this book to be useful in any way, please tell your friends, family, and colleagues about it. Also, do share this information with anyone you feel can use to help with their weight. After all, we all need help at some point. So, this book will hopefully offer them the opportunity to make the most of their effort.

Thank you once again for choosing this book. There are plenty of other options out there. By selecting this book, you have given us the motivation to continue doing our best to help others improve their lives and well-being.

CPSIA information can be obtained
at www.ICGtesting.com
Printed in the USA
BVHW040952200521
R12259400001B/R122594PG607359BVX00003B/3